THE REVIVE CAFE COOKBOOK 5

www.revive.co.nz

Copyright ✪ Revive Concepts Limited 2015
Published by Revive Concepts Limited
First printing 2015 (this book).

ISBN: 978-0-473-32655-5

Also by Jeremy Dixon: The Revive Cafe Cookbook
                       The Revive Cafe Cookbook 2
                       The Revive Cafe Cookbook 3
                       The Revive Cafe Cookbook 4
                       Cook:30 Cookbook

Produced in New Zealand. Printed in China.
Food Preparation, Styling & Photography: Jeremy Dixon
Cafe Photography: Elesha Newton
Graphic Design: Rebecca Zwitser, Jeremy Dixon
Proof Reader: Nyree Tomkins
Recipe testing: Nyree Tomkins, Elesha Newton, Narelle Liggett, Keryn McCutcheon, Annelise Greenfield, Kirsten Ockleston, Dyanne Dixon, Elisabeth Tupai
Proofing: Verity Dixon, Dawn Simpson, Annelise Greenfield, Chad Bishop, Kjirstnne Jensen, Heather Cameron

The publisher makes no guarantee as to the availability of the products in this book. Every effort has been made to ensure the accuracy of the information presented and any claims made; however, it is the responsibility of the reader to ensure the suitability of the product and recipe for their particular needs. Many natural ingredients vary in size and texture, and differences in raw ingredients may marginally affect the outcome of some dishes. Recipes from the cafes have been adjusted to make them more appropriate for a home kitchen. All health advice given in this book is a guideline only. Professional medical or nutritional advice should be sought for any specific issues.

Metric and imperial measurements have been used in this cookbook. The tablespoon size used is 15ml (½fl oz), teaspoon 5ml (⅙fl oz) and cup 250ml (8fl oz). Some countries use slightly different sized measurements, however these should not make a significant difference to the outcome of the recipes.

Revive Cafes   Contact Details:
24 Wyndham St, Auckland Central, New Zealand   P O Box 12-887, Penrose, Auckland 1642, New Zealand
33 Lorne St, Auckland Central, New Zealand   Email: info@revive.co.nz   Phone: +64-9-303 0420

If you like the recipes in this book I recommend you sign up for my weekly inspirational Revive e-mails.
They contain a weekly recipe, cooking and lifestyle tips, the weekly Revive menu, special offers and Revive news.
Visit www.revive.co.nz to sign up or to purchase more copies of this or our other cookbooks online.
Privacy Policy: Revive will never share your details and you can unsubscribe at any time.
LIKE us on Facebook to get more recipes and health tips! www.facebook.com/cafe.revive.

the *revive* cafe cookbook 5

Contents

Revive Cafe Update 7

Cookbook Notes. 8

Essentials 10

The 8 Keys to Healthy Living 12

Salads 15

Hotpots & Stir Fries 41

Main Meals 75

Soups 101

Sides. 117

Flavour Boosters 129

Breakfasts. 143

Sweet Things 161

Step-by-Step 177

Quick Guide (Cooking Grains, Beans & Lentils) 186

Cookbook Series Reference Guide 188

Recipe Index. 190

Revive Cafe Update

This year, on 14 February 2015, Revive turned 10 years old! It has been an amazing journey since I opened the doors of Revive at my first cafe in Fort St, Auckland Central.

I always remember my first 3 customers. Well, they were actually the first 3 people that came through the door.

I had spent all my savings and 2 months preparing this new cafe. Painting, menu development and getting good staff. My life dream was about to become a reality. I opened the doors to the cafe. Everything was new and I was brimming with anticipation of what was to come.

The first person through the door came up to the counter and asked "Can I please have a latte?" I had decided that Revive cafe would be truly healthy and not serve coffee. I explained that we do not have coffees, and they quickly exited to find another cafe.

The second person came up and said "Can I please have a flat white?" I thought I would be more strategic and suggested they have a healthy smoothie or juice instead. They of course were after a caffeine fix, politely declined and quickly exited.

The third person came in and again coffee was requested. I said that we did not serve coffee and was about to start my new line on upgrading them to a juice or smoothie when he shouted at me "What? A cafe without coffee! Are you some kind of religious nut or something?" and stormed out.

I was devastated. What a start to this new adventure for which I had put everything on the line! However it turned out ok and within a short time I had people queuing out the door to eat this healthy new food.

Over the next 2 years I went through the "dip" trying different offerings, staffing levels, pricing and marketing until I found a concept that was popular and financially viable. And 10 years later Revive is going strong and we serve over 100,000 meals and salads a year across my 2 branches in Auckland Central.

The other highlight of the past year was being invited to do a cooking show for a 3ABN, a US satellite Christian TV channel. I travelled to Illinois to film 26 episodes of a new programme called Cook:30. Here I show how I cook a multi-course Revive-style meal in my own home, doing everything from scratch ... in just 30 minutes. Check out www.revive.co.nz to view some of the episodes. I also produced a cookbook to go along with the programme that has a chapter for each episode. It repeats many of the recipes from my cookbooks 1-4 so is like a "best of" cookbook.

It is exciting to see how my vision 10 years ago has grown from cafes to cookbooks to TV!

I hope you enjoy these new recipes in this fifth cookbook of mine. I am constantly amazed how I actually come up with more recipes! People always ask me how I get my recipes and I actually do not know. I just try a new dish or two each week and photograph it. And I eventually have enough to make another cookbook. It is great to be able to share how healthy cooking can be easy and delicious.

Eat healthy and follow the 8 keys to healthy living and you will have more energy and vitality and your chances of getting nasty diseases are significantly reduced. LIfe is too short to not live it 100%!

Jeremy Dixon
June 2015

Cookbook Notes

Garlic, Ginger & Chilli

Garlic and ginger have amazing flavour-enhancing properties and we use both extensively at Revive and in these recipes.   Simply chop them up finely before adding to a dish or you can make your own purees by blending the garlic or ginger with a little oil.   You can get pureed ginger from most supermarkets.

I recommend that garlic should always be used fresh and never purchased in a puree as it has an unpleasant flavour. You can also buy pre-crushed/pureed chilli in a jar which is used in some recipes.

Sweeteners

The recipes do not use added refined sugar. The most convenient natural sweetener is liquid honey. Alternatively make up a batch of date puree (page 139) which is an excellent and inexpensive sweetener.

There are also other healthy sweeteners available such as apple sauce, agave and maple syrup.

Nuts

Nuts are used in many dishes at Revive and in this cookbook. Unless specified, raw nuts are used. However, having the wrong sort of nut will not affect the outcome of most recipes as they are usually interchangeable. You can use nut pieces if you want to minimise cost. Roasted nuts are usually used where they are presented whole (in salads or stir fries) so they hold their crunchiness and do not go soggy.

Oils

My favourite oils are rice bran, olive, coconut and grapeseed. Wherever a recipe calls for oil you can use any of these, whichever is your favourite.

Beans/Chickpeas

I have used tinned beans/chickpeas (garbanzo beans) in all of the recipes as this is the most convenient. Drain all tins before using.

If you can use freshly cooked beans they will taste better and are significantly cheaper. 1 tin of beans is around 2 cups.

I recommend that you soak and cook your own beans and store them in your freezer. You will need to soak overnight in plenty of water (they expand three times their volume). Then cook in fresh water until soft, which will be between 30 minutes and 2 hours, depending on the bean and its age. Then freeze them in small containers for easy use.

To defrost, simply run some hot water over them in a sieve or colander for 30 seconds.

Thickeners

I use arrowroot for thickening sauces and desserts in the recipes in this book. You can use cornflour (cornstarch) instead however you may need to use more and you may get a whiter colour.

Creams

Different methods are used to make some dishes creamy. Coconut cream, almond cream and cashew cream can usually be used interchangeably.

Cooking Grains

I recommend that you cook extra grains like rice and quinoa and store in your refrigerator for an easy ingredient to use in the following few days. When you cook grains remember to use boiling water to save time, and first bring the grain to the boil before turning down to a simmer. Do not stir while cooking and keep the lid on.

Cooking Terms

Saute: to cook food on a high heat and in a little oil while stirring with a wooden spoon.
Simmer: to have food cooking at a low heat setting so it is just bubbling.
Roast: to bake in the oven covered with a little oil. Use fan bake setting to achieve more even cooking.

Mixing

You can mix most recipes in the pot you are cooking in or in a big mixing bowl. When mixing, stir gently so as not to damage the food. With salads, mix with your hands if possible. Gently lift up the ingredients and let them fall down with gravity rather than squeezing.

Peeling Vegetables

If in good clean condition, I do not peel potatoes, carrots or kumara. You gain extra vitamins, higher yield and save plenty of time.

Tahini

This is a great ingredient for dressings made from ground sesame seeds, kind of like runnier peanut butter. Make sure you get hulled tahini.

Taste Test

It is difficult to get a recipe that works 100% the same every time, especially when you are using natural and fresh ingredients. Sizes in vegetables vary, spices and herbs differ in strength and you can even get differences in evaporation rates with different sized pots. Make sure you taste test every dish before you serve and be willing to add more seasoning or a little more cooking time if necessary.

Blenders

Some recipes require a food processor (usually with an S blade). Other recipes require a blender or liquidiser (usually a tall jug with 4 pronged blades) or stick blender. Some hotpots require a stick blender to blend the mixture to make it smoother and more consistent, but if you don't have one don't worry as this will not alter the outcome significantly.

Quantities

The quantities for each dish are an estimate and will vary depending on cooking times and ingredient size. I have used one cup as an average serving size.

Gluten Free & Dairy Free

A large proportion of the recipes are gluten free and/ or dairy free. If you have any allergies you will need to check that each recipe is suitable.

Essentials Fridge & Freezer

Freeze and refrigerate leftovers and cooked grains/beans. Regularly stock up basic produce as required and as in season.

Freezer

berries: boysenberries, blueberries, strawberries, raspberries

cooked beans: chickpeas (garbanzo), red kidney, white, black, black-eye

corn kernels

peas

red capsicum (bell peppers) diced

spinach (usually in pieces)

Refrigerator

aioli (page 138) or tahini dressing (page 141)

almond butter

basil pesto (page 139)

crushed chilli (puree)

date puree (page 139)

ginger puree

hummus or other dips

leftover rice or quinoa

relish

soy sauce

sweet chilli sauce

Thai curry pastes: red, green, yellow, Massaman, Penang

Produce

beetroot

broccoli

cabbage: red, white

carrots

cauliflower

celery

cucumber, telegraph

fruit: bananas, lemons, apples

garlic

herbs: mint, parsley, basil, coriander (cilantro)

kumara (sweet potato): red, orange, gold

leeks

lettuce: cos (romaine), iceberg, fancy, mesclun

mesclun lettuce

mushrooms

onions: brown, red

potatoes

pumpkin

silver beet (Swiss chard)

spring onions (scallions)

tomatoes

zucchini (courgette)

Essentials Pantry

These items are shelf stable and generally have a long life. Always keep these stocked up so you can use at any time.

Herbs & Spices

coriander

cumin

curry powder

mixed herbs

smoked paprika

thyme

turmeric

General

tinned chopped tomatoes

chickpea (besan/chana) flour

coconut cream

dried fruit: sultanas, raisins, prunes, dates, apricots

honey

oil: rice bran, olive, sesame

olives: kalamata, black

pasta and pasta sheets

peanut butter, tahini (sesame seed paste)

soy sauce or tamari

vinegar: balsamic, cider

whole grain mustard

Grains

brown rice : long grain, short grain

bulghur wheat

couscous: fine, Israeli

quinoa

rolled oats: fine, jumbo

Beans

tinned and dried beans: chickpeas (garbanzo), red kidney, white, black, black-eyed

dried lentils: red, yellow, brown (crimson), green

Nuts & Seeds

almonds

Brazil nuts

cashew nuts

poppy seeds

sesame seeds: black, white

shredded coconut

sunflower seeds

The 8 Keys to Healthy Living

These are the health principles that Revive is founded on. To have complete energy and vitality, it is not enough to just eat healthy food. There are other simple things that create good health, summarised by these 8 keys.

The good news is that if you apply these 8 simple steps in your day-to-day living, you will notice dramatic improvements in your vitality, health and quality of life.

1. Nutrition - eat plant-based foods, fresh produce and avoid processed foods and sugars.

2. Exercise - get at least 30 minutes every day.

3. Water - drink at least 2 litres (2 quarts) of pure water per day.

4. Sunshine - aim for 10 minutes minimum per day.

5. Temperance - free yourself from stimulants like alcohol, energy drinks, coffee and drugs.

6. Air - breathe deeply - start every day with 10 deep breaths.

7. Rest - get 8 hours quality sleep every night.

8. Trust - live at peace with everyone and your God.

...tion

Exercise

Water

Sunshine

...erance

Air

Rest

Trust

Salads

Bright Butter Beans 16

Pesto Green Beans 18

Mexican Guacamole Salad 20

Tropical Summer Salad 22

Parsnip, Pear, Rocket & Pecans 24

Watercress & Potato Salad 26

Purple Power Quinoa Salad 28

Thai Green Curry Rice 30

Tangy Fennel Tofu Salad 32

Autumn Butternut Salad 34

Asian Cabbage Crunch 36

Pineapple Powered Sweet Potato 38

White beans have a lovely creamy taste and this is an excellent bean salad. Using the three rules of salad making, colour, colour and colour this is a lovely salad. The crunchiness of the celery and capsicum make this salad nice and fresh.

Bright Butter Beans

MAKES 6 X 1 CUP SERVES

2 x 400g (12oz) tins
butter beans

2 cups cherry
tomatoes halved

1 cup celery
roughly chopped

1 cup green capsicum (bell
pepper) roughly diced

½ cup olives pitted

½ teaspoon salt

¼ cup red onion

¼ cup vinaigrette

VINAIGRETTE

2 tablespoons oil

1 tablespoon lemon juice

1 teaspoon apple
cider vinegar

2 teaspoons honey

¼ teaspoon salt

¼ cup Italian parsley
finely chopped

1 clove garlic crushed or
finely chopped

1. Combine the vinaigrette ingredients in a small bowl or cup and stir.

2. Combine the salad ingredients in a large bowl and pour over the vinaigrette.

Use any combination of beans and colourful vegetables.

This is a lovely simple salad bursting with freshness. Make your own pesto for a healthier lower cost option.

Pesto Green Beans

MAKES 5 X 1 CUP SERVES

3 cups green beans

1 cup cherry
tomatoes halved

1 cup kalamata olives pitted

½ cup basil pesto
(page 139)

garnish: handful of fresh
basil leaves

1. Cut the ends off the beans and cook in a pot of boiling water for 4 minutes. Drain and soak in cold water to stop cooking.

2. Mix the basil pesto with the beans and place on serving plate.

3. Add the olives and tomatoes on top.

4. Garnish with some more fresh basil.

To save time you can use supermarket-bought pesto.

You can also just soak the beans in boiling water to cook - although it may take longer.

Basil Pesto

This delicious dressing is the most aromatic salad addition around. You can buy it in the supermarket or make your own with the recipe on page 139.

I love Mexican food and I love avocado. So here is a salad that combines them all.

Mexican Guacamole Salad

MAKES 8 X 1 CUP SERVES

2 cups frozen corn or 400g (12oz) tin whole corn

400g (12oz) tin black beans

1 orange capsicum (bell pepper) finely cubed

1½ cups cherry tomatoes quartered

½ cup spring onions finely sliced (around 1 large)

3 cups cos lettuce finely sliced

GUACAMOLE DRESSING:

1 cup fresh coriander

1 large avocado mashed

2 tablespoons lime juice

2 tablespoons lemon juice

1 tablespoon honey or date puree

½ teaspoon salt

3 tablespoons oil

3 cloves garlic finely chopped or crushed

1. Put the corn into a sieve and briefly run some hot water through it to defrost. Put the corn into your serving bowl.

2. Put the rest of the salad ingredients into the bowl.

3. Put the dressing ingredients into a small bowl and mix well. Pour over the salad ingredients and mix through gently.

If you like a little heat you can add some finely diced chilli peppers.

Fruit in salads do not usually sell well at Revive so we would not have this in the salad bar. But it is a really refreshing and colourful salad to have with savoury items.

Tropical Summer Salad

MAKES 6 X 1 CUP SERVES

2 cups watermelon diced

1 cup cucumber diced

2 cups paw paw (papaya) diced

2 tablespoons lime juice

garnish: mint

garnish: limes

1. Chop fruit and arrange on your serving dish.

2. Drizzle lime juice over the top and garnish with mint leaves and extra limes.

Use a sharp knife and handle chopped fruit gently so you maintain crisp edges.

Paw Paw/Papaya

A lovely tropical fruit. Adding lime juice transforms the flavour into something amazing. Great for fruit salads.

Parsnip, Pear, Rocket & Pecans

MAKES 5 X 1 CUP SERVES

2 large parsnips sliced
3mm (⅛in)

1 teaspoon oil

2 cups baby rocket (rucola)
or other baby greens

1 pear cored and sliced
long-ways

½ cup golden raisins

½ cup pecan nuts

1 tablespoon coconut slivers

2 tablespoons mint
finely chopped

1. In a bowl mix the parsnip and oil together. Put onto an oven tray and
    bake at 180°C (350°F) for around 15 minutes or until just getting soft.

2. Combine all ingredients in a bowl and mix.

Slice the parsnip evenly so you get even cooking.

Pecan Nuts

These are a lovely nut to use in salads. They are in my "expensive"
nut range so just use them sparingly. A handful on a salad can really
transform it. To make them go further you can chop them into quarters.

This is a salad that was on the menu in our first week when I started Revive in 2005. Unfortunately the hazelnuts were too expensive and watercress was not reliably available every day so it did not feature permanently on our menu, however it is a nice salad to have for special occasions.

Watercress & Potato Salad

MAKES 8 X 1 CUP SERVES

4 cups small potatoes cubed

2 teaspoons oil

4 cups watercress roughly chopped

½ cup mint roughly chopped

1 red capsicum (bell pepper) thinly sliced

½ cup roasted hazelnuts

½ cup honey mustard dressing

garnish: mint

HONEY MUSTARD DRESSING:

2 tablespoons seeded mustard

1 tablespoon honey

½ teaspoon salt

3 tablespoons lemon juice

3 tablespoons tahini

1. In a bowl mix the potatoes and oil together. Put onto an oven tray and bake at 180°C (350°F) for 20 minutes or until just getting soft.

2. In a cup mix the dressing.

3. In a bowl mix the potatoes with the dressing.

4. Put the watercress and mint on your serving dish. Add the potatoes and top with the capsicum and hazelnuts.

5. Garnish with some extra mint.

To make expensive whole nuts go further you can chop them into smaller pieces or buy them as pieces.

If watercress is not available you can replace with baby spinach or a mesclun lettuce mix.

Hazelnuts

A lovely nut that is especially delicious when roasted. While these are expensive nuts you do not need to use many of them.

Purple is the colour I try to have in my salad bar every week at Revive. The spread of colourful salads never looks complete when purple is missing. So I thought I would go to the extreme and create a salad full of purple ingredients.

Purple Power Quinoa Salad

MAKES 5 X 1 CUP SERVES

¾ cup white quinoa

1½ cups boiling water

1 cup beetroot julienne (around ½ large beetroot)

1 cup purple cabbage thinly sliced

1 cup purple grapes

½ cup radishes cut into half moons

garnish: coriander (cilantro)

DRESSING

2 tablespoons oil

1 teaspoon apple cider vinegar

1 tablespoon honey or date puree

1 tablespoon seeded mustard

¾ teaspoon salt

2 teaspoons lime juice

1. In a pot combine the quinoa and boiling water and heat to bring back to the boil. Turn down to low and simmer with the lid on for 12 minutes or until the water has gone and the quinoa is soft. This should yield 2 cups of cooked quinoa.

2. Chop all the vegetables and put into a mixing bowl.

3. Mix the dressing ingredients in a cup.

4. Combine the cooked quinoa with the vegetables and dressing and mix well so the beetroot colours the salad.

5. Serve and garnish with fresh coriander and some lime wedges.

You can also use red quinoa for even more purple power!

Apple Cider Vinegar

I am not a big fan of vinegar as it can have a very strong flavour. But a little tartness in a dressing can just lift it and make all the flavours wonderfully mingle together. I prefer apple cider vinegar to most other vinegars. You can use lemon juice if you do not like vinegar.

MAKES 6 X 1 CUP SERVES

1½ cups long grain brown rice

3 cups boiling water

2 cups broccoli florets

4 cups boiling water

1 cup red capsicum (bell pepper) roughly diced

1 cup frozen peas

½ cup bamboo shoots (fine)

½ cup fresh coriander (cilantro) chopped

garnish: coriander (cilantro)

garnish: peanuts chopped

DRESSING:

1 teaspoon ginger puree or finely chopped

2 tablespoons honey or date puree

165ml (5oz) tin coconut cream (small tin)

1 tablespoon Thai green curry paste

1 teaspoon salt

1 tablespoon finely chopped lemongrass (fresh or frozen)

I originally had this recipe planned for my first recipe book but it was taken out at the last minute due to space and the original photo was not that great. I only recently remembered it was missed out and had to include it as it is one of our most popular rice salads at Revive.

Thai Green Curry Rice

1. In a pot combine the rice and boiling water and heat to bring back to the boil. Turn down to low and simmer with the lid on for 20 minutes or until the water has gone and the rice is soft. This should yield 4 cups of cooked rice.

2. Cut the broccoli and cook in a pot with the boiling water for 3 minutes. When finished immediately rinse with cold water to stop the cooking.

3. Mix the dressing ingredients together in a small bowl.

4. Combine all ingredients and stir through the dressing.

I find different curry pastes can have different heat levels. Start with 1 tablespoon of curry paste in this recipe and taste. Sometimes you may need to add 1-2 more tablespoons of curry paste to get the best intensity of flavour.

Bamboo Shoots

A great Thai ingredient that will work pretty much every time you use a Thai curry paste. They are fairly tasteless but give a nice texture. They come in tins. I prefer the matchstick sized ones but you can also get them in larger sizes too. Available from Asian stores and most supermarkets.

This is a "combine random ingredients in the fridge" type of recipe. I thought this would be a side dish when I started making it. However I kept adding ingredients and it just kept growing into a tasty salad.

Tangy Fennel Tofu Salad

MAKES 3 X 1 CUP SERVES

1 cup fennel root sliced thinly (around 1 bulb)

2 cloves garlic finely chopped or crushed

2 teaspoons oil

300g (12oz) firm tofu cut into small pieces

¼ cup red onion finely diced (around ¼ onion)

½ teaspoon finely chopped fresh red chilli

1½ cups frozen peas

1 teaspoon celery seeds

½ teaspoon salt

2 tablespoons lemon juice

garnish: mint leaves

garnish: lemon wedge

1. In a pot or pan saute the fennel, garlic and oil for around 5 minutes or until the fennel is soft.

2. Add the tofu, red onion, chilli, peas, celery seeds and salt and cook for another 5 minutes stirring regularly until the tofu is browning.

3. Stir through lemon juice just before serving.

4. Serve with extra lemon slices.

Don't rub your eyes after handling chilli. I did and it hurts!!!

Fennel

Fennel is kind of like a big fat short celery root with a lovely flavour. It is nice raw in salads and goes sweet like celery when sauted. It is not something you will use all the time, but if you see it on special at your produce shop give it a go for something different! Just slice the tough root end off (like you would with celery) and slice it into strips.

I originally planned this salad to have an olive dressing over it. Fortunately I took some photos before adding the dressing as it totally ruined the look of the salad. It tasted awesome, but was not cookbook quality. I thought I would include it just as it is with no dressing. The ingredients are so flavoursome no dressing is actually needed for this combination. So the olive dressing in the flavour boosters section of this book is optional.

Autumn Butternut Salad

MAKES 8 X 1 CUP SERVES

2 cups butternut squash or pumpkin chopped into 2cm (1in) cubes

2 teaspoons oil

100g (3oz) baby spinach

½ cup mint
roughly chopped

1 cup cherry tomatoes

1 large avocado cubed

1. In a bowl mix the butternut and oil together. Put onto an oven tray and bake at 180°C (350°F) for around 20 minutes or until just getting soft.

2. Lay down the spinach and mint on your serving dish.

3. Put all other ingredients on top.

Roasted Butternut

This is the most awesome ingredient you can add to a salad or hotpot (or almost any meal). Just roast in the oven with a little oil and it comes up sweet and soft and delicious. You can also leave the skin on as it will become soft too! You can use other pumpkin varieties too.

This is a nice simple salad to make and people who do not like coleslaw (raw cabbage salad) will most likely like it!

Asian Cabbage Crunch

MAKES 8 X 1 CUP SERVES

10 cups white cabbage roughly sliced (around ½ medium cabbage)

1 cup spring onions (scallions) sliced (around 3)

2 cloves garlic crushed

1 teaspoon sesame oil

1 tablespoon oil

½ teaspoon salt

garnish: 2 tablespoons sliced almonds

garnish: 1 tablespoon sesame seeds

garnish: 1 tablespoon shredded coconut

1. In a pot or pan saute the cabbage, spring onions, garlic and oil for 5 minutes or until the cabbage is just starting to get soft.

2. Add the salt and stir.

3. Put onto the serving dish garnished with almonds, sesame seeds and coconut.

Cooked Cabbage

If you do not like cabbage make sure you try it lightly cooked. It gets soft and loses the harsh flavour that it has when it is raw. You can steam it or fry it. And of course make sure you add some interesting flavours and a little salt.

I love roasted vegetable salads. This one is great with a lovely pineapple dressing!

Pineapple Powered Sweet Potato

MAKES 8 X 1 CUP SERVES

6 cups red kumara (sweet potato) chopped into 2cm (1in) cubes (around 2 large kumara)

4 cups carrots chopped into 1cm (½in) cubes (around 4 large carrots)

1 tablespoon curry powder

½ teaspoon salt

1 tablespoon oil

1 cup red capsicum (bell pepper) finely diced

garnish: parsley

DRESSING:

200g (6oz) tin pineapple in juice

2 tablespoons lemon juice

1. In a bowl mix the kumara, carrots, curry powder, salt and oil together. Put onto an oven tray and bake at 180°C (350°F) for around 20 minutes or until just getting soft.

2. Put the dressing ingredients into a blender and blend.

3. Mix the roasted vegetables, capsicum and the dressing.

4. Serve garnished with parsley.

It is important that the carrots and kumara are soft. Test them before you take them out of the oven. A good test is making sure you can squash them easily with your thumb or a fork. Or you can just try a piece.

Crushed Pineapple

This is an excellent ingredient to have in tins in your pantry. It adds excellent instant sweetness and flavour to many salads, hotpots and sweet dishes. Make sure you buy the pineapple in "natural juice" not in a syrup that is loaded with refined sugar.

Hotpots & Stir Fries

Sri Lankin Balti 42

South Indian Eggplant & Cashew Curry 44

Chickpea Tikka Masala 46

Dahl Aloo Ghobi 48

Lentil Ragout on Potato Mash 50

Tamarind & Butternut Dahl 52

Chana Saag 54

Mexican Black Bean Casserole 56

Quinoa Stir Fry with Tempeh 58

Hot Mushroom Mingle 60

Thai Vegetable Stir Fry 62

Thai Green Curry Tofu 64

Thai Kumara Stir Fry 66

Satay Wild Rice Risotto 68

Amaranth & Root Vege Mingle 70

MAKES 6 X 1 CUP SERVES

4 cups pumpkin or butternut squash chopped into 2cm (1in) cubes

2 teaspoons oil (bake)

2 teaspoons oil (saute)

1½ cups onion finely diced (around 1 onion)

2 cloves garlic finely chopped or crushed

1 tablespoon ginger puree or finely chopped

½ teaspoon cardamom powder

optional: ½ teaspoon fenugreek powder

1 teaspoon clove powder

2 tablespoons honey or date puree

2 x 400g (12oz) tins chopped tomatoes

1 teaspoon salt

2 tablespoons tomato paste

450g (15oz) tofu frozen and defrosted

200ml (6oz) coconut cream

garnish: roughly chopped fresh coriander (cilantro)

I love using frozen tofu in hotpots and it is a great way to serve up a dish to people who normally eat chicken. While they may not necessarily be fooled, it is a nice way to add some interesting protein texture.

Sri Lankin Balti

1. In a bowl mix the pumpkin and oil together. Put onto an oven tray and bake at 180°C (350°F) for around 15 minutes or until just getting soft.

2. In a pot or pan saute the oil, onion, garlic and ginger for 5 minutes or until the onion is soft.

3. Add the spices and stir for around 30 seconds to activate the flavours.

4. Add the honey, tomatoes, salt and tomato paste and heat until it is just bubbling.

5. Tear strips off the block of tofu that has been frozen and defrosted. Add to the curry.

6. Add the cooked pumpkin and stir in the coconut cream.

7. Garnish with coriander and serve on brown rice, wholemeal couscous, wholemeal pasta or quinoa.

Torn Tofu

This is a different way to prepare tofu. First drain any water and freeze for at least 2 days. Defrost overnight in the fridge, or for 15 minutes in a bowl of boiling water. Tear off bite sized strips and add to any curry!

The real reason I created this dish was I had bought this lovely purple pot that I just had to use in my next cookbook. What food is purple? Eggplant! That is a good start and then I remembered an eggplant curry I had years ago at an Indian restaurant. So this Indian Eggplant Curry using cashew cream was born.

South Indian Eggplant & Cashew Curry

MAKES 6 X 1 CUP SERVES

8 cups eggplant (aubergine) chopped into 1cm (½in) cubes (around 2 eggplant)

1 tablespoon oil (bake)

1 cup onion finely diced (around 1 medium onion)

2 cloves garlic finely chopped or crushed

1 tablespoon ginger puree or finely chopped

1 teaspoon oil (saute)

1 tablespoon coriander ground

2 tablespoons honey or date puree

1 teaspoon tamarind paste

400g (12oz) tin crushed tomatoes

1 teaspoon salt

½ cup cashew nuts

1 cup water

garnish: whole cashew nuts

garnish: fresh coriander (cilantro)

1. In a bowl mix the eggplant and oil together. Put onto an oven tray and bake at 180°C (350°F) for around 15 minutes or until just getting soft.

2. In a pot or pan saute the onion, garlic, ginger in the oil for around 5 minutes or until the onion is soft.

3. Add the coriander and stir for 30 seconds to activate the flavours.

4. Add the honey, tamarind, tomatoes and salt and heat until nearly bubbling.

5. Put the cashew nuts and water into a blender and blend until you have a smooth milk. Add to the curry.

6. Add the cooked eggplant.

7. Serve garnished with cashew nuts and fresh coriander.

Tamarind Paste

Tamarind is a bitter apricot. It usually comes as a tamarind paste which has a sour and slightly bitter taste but goes well in some Indian curries. Each batch can be different so start sparingly and add more after tasting if necessary. It is available from Indian supermarkets and some whole food stores.

This is a lovely Indian dish that is usually served with chicken. Here is a healthier version with chickpeas instead.

Chickpea Tikka Masala

MAKES 8 X 1 CUP SERVES

2 cups red kumara (sweet potato) chopped into 2cm (1in) cubes (unpeeled)

2 teaspoons oil (bake)

2 teaspoons oil (saute)

1½ cups onion finely diced (around 1 onion)

2 cloves garlic finely chopped or crushed

1 tablespoon ginger puree or finely chopped

1 teaspoon cumin

1 teaspoon smoked paprika

½ teaspoon clove powder

½ teaspoon turmeric

⅛ teaspoon chilli powder

1 tablespoon honey or date puree

½ teaspoon salt

2 x 400g (12oz) tins chopped tomatoes

6 tablespoons tomato paste

2 x 400g (12oz) tins chickpeas (garbanzo beans)

200g (6oz) coconut cream

garnish: fresh coriander (cilantro)

serve with: cooked brown rice garnished with almonds

1. In a bowl mix the kumara and oil together. Put onto an oven tray and bake at 180°C (350°F) for around 15 minutes or until just getting soft.

2. In a pot or pan saute the oil, onion and garlic for 5 minutes or until the onion is soft.

3. Add the spices and stir around for 30 seconds to activate the flavours.

4. Add the honey, salt, tomatoes and tomato paste and heat until just bubbling. Blend the mixture with a stick blender until smooth.

5. Add the chickpeas, coconut cream and cooked kumara.

6. Drizzle a little coconut cream on top of the dish and lightly stir in. Garnish with coriander.

7. Serve with brown rice garnished with sliced almonds.

Dahls are very quick to cook as red lentils cook in under 15 minutes. This is a lovely dahl with potato (aloo) and cauliflower (ghobi). You can substitute other vegetables and it will still taste delicious.

Dahl Aloo Ghobi

MAKES 8 X 1 CUP SERVES

4 cups potato chopped into 2cm (1in) cubes

2 teaspoons oil (bake)

3 cups cauliflower cut into small florets

2 teaspoons oil (saute)

1½ cups onion finely diced (around 1 onion)

4 cloves garlic finely chopped or crushed

2 tablespoons ginger puree or finely chopped

1 cup red capsicum (bell pepper) roughly diced (around 1)

2 tablespoons brown or yellow mustard seeds

2 tablespoons cumin seeds

1 tablespoon coriander powder

1 teaspoon turmeric

1 cup red lentils

4 cups boiling water

1 tablespoon honey or date puree

1 teaspoon salt

1 tablespoon sweet chilli sauce

½ cup raw cashew nuts

1 cup cold water

serve with: brown rice

garnish: fresh coriander (cilantro)

1. In a bowl mix the potato and oil together. Put onto an oven tray and bake at 180°C (350°F) for 30 minutes or until just getting soft.

2. Put the cauliflower in a pot with some boiling water and cook for 5 minutes or until just starting to get soft. Drain immediately.

3. In a pot or pan saute the oil, onion, garlic, ginger, capsicum and seeds for 5 minutes or until the onion is soft and the seeds start to pop.

4. Stir in the coriander and turmeric for around 30 seconds to activate the flavours.

5. Add the lentils and boiling water and simmer for 15 minutes or until the lentils are soft.

6. Add the honey, salt and sweet chilli sauce.

7. Blend the cashew nuts and water together into a runny cream and add to the dahl.

8. Add the cooked potato and cauliflower.

9. Serve on brown rice with a garnish of coriander.

So many of my hotpot recipes are served on brown rice - which is awesome. However I thought my book needed to have another option. This ragout goes really well on this potato mash and is a great comforting winter warming meal.

Lentil Ragout on Potato Mash

MAKES 5 X 1 CUP SERVES

¾ cup brown lentils

3 cups boiling water

1 tablespoon oil

1½ cups onion finely diced (around 1 onion)

3 cloves garlic finely chopped or crushed

2 cups eggplant (aubergine) diced (around 1 large)

15 button mushrooms cut in half

2 cups chopped courgettes (zucchini) (around 2 medium)

1 teaspoon mixed herbs

2 tablespoons soy sauce

½ teaspoon salt

2 teaspoons arrowroot or 3 teaspoons cornflour

1 cup hot water

POTATO MASH

MAKES 5 X 1 CUP SERVES

1kg (2lb) washed potatoes roughly cubed

2 litres (4 quarts) boiling water

½ cup milk of your choice

½ teaspoon salt

2 tablespoons chopped parsley

garnish: rosemary

1. In a pot combine the lentils and boiling water and bring back to the boil. Turn down to low and simmer with the lid on for 30 minutes or until the lentils are soft. This should yield 2 cups of cooked lentils. Alternatively use canned lentils.

2. In a pot or pan saute the oil, onion, garlic, eggplant, mushrooms, courgettes and mixed herbs for around 10 minutes or until the mixture is soft.

3. In a cup mix the soy sauce, salt, arrowroot and hot water. Pour into the ragout and stir until it is well mixed. Add the cooked lentils and stir in.

4. You may need to add some more water, or cook for a little longer to achieve the correct consistency.

5. Put the potatoes and boiling water into a pot and simmer for around 15 minutes or until soft. Mash well and mix in the milk, salt and parsley.

6. Serve the potatoes onto the plate and create a well. Spoon the ragout into the middle and garnish with some fresh rosemary.

At Revive we used to rotate hotpots and had one hotpot per day. However the dahls were so popular I just wanted to repeat them all the time. Shortly after we moved from our Fort St store to Wyndham St in 2013 we decided to make dahls their own dish and from then on we offered hotpots and dahls as different options. Lentils taste great when cooked well with interesting ingredients and are a great protein source. This dish is one of the dahls we serve at Revive.

Tamarind & Butternut Dahl

MAKES 7 X 1 CUP SERVES

4 cups pumpkin or butternut squash chopped into 2cm (1in) cubes

2 teaspoons oil (bake)

2 teaspoons oil (saute)

1½ cups onion finely diced (around 1 onion)

2 teaspoons fenugreek powder (optional)

⅛ teaspoon chilli powder (optional)

3 cloves garlic finely chopped or crushed

1 cup brown (crimson) lentils

5 cups boiling water

1 tablespoon honey or date puree

¾ teaspoon salt

4 tablespoons tomato paste

1 tablespoon tamarind paste

200ml (6oz) coconut cream

garnish: fresh coriander

1. In a bowl mix the pumpkin and oil together. Put onto an oven tray and bake at 180°C (350°F) for around 15 minutes or until just getting soft.

2. In a pot or pan saute the oil, onion, fenugreek, chilli and garlic for 5 minutes or until the onion is soft.

3. Add the lentils and boiling water, bring back to the boil, and simmer for 20 minutes or until the lentils are soft. You may have to add a little more water if it dries out before the lentils are cooked.

4. Add the honey, salt, tomato paste, tamarind and heat until nearly bubbling.

5. Add the coconut cream (reserve some for garnish) and stir through.

6. Serve with a garnish of coconut cream and fresh coriander on brown rice.

You can find tamarind paste at most Indian stores.

This dish will thicken as it cools, if it is too runny just cook for another 5 minutes.

This is a dish appearing on most Indian restaurant menus - usually near the bottom as I guess most people do not want to order it. It usually comes with a lot of cream and paneer (a type of cheese). This healthy version uses chickpeas and is fresh and delicious!

Chana Saag

MAKES 6 X 1 CUP SERVES

1½ cups onion finely diced (around 1 onion)

3 cloves garlic finely chopped or crushed

1 tablespoon ginger puree or finely chopped

1 tablespoon oil

1 tablespoon cumin

1 tablespoon coriander

5 cups frozen spinach (around 600g (20oz))

½ teaspoon salt

200g (6oz) coconut cream

2 x 400g (12oz) tins chickpeas (garbanzo beans)

garnish: red capsicum (bell pepper) finely chopped

1. In a pot or pan saute the onion, garlic, ginger and oil for 5 minutes or until the onion is soft.

2. Add the spices and stir for 30 seconds to activate the flavours.

3. Add the frozen spinach and heat for 5-10 minutes until it is soft.

4. Add the salt and coconut cream.

5. Blend the mixture using a stick blender, or by putting it all into a blender. Make sure you blend it well, you do not want any stringy bits.

6. Put back in the pan or pot, add the chickpeas and heat until just bubbling.

7. Serve with a garnish of some finely chopped red capsicum.

Spinach can turn a black colour when overcooked. Make sure you add spinach near the end and serve soon after cooking.

I love the comforting and hearty flavour of black beans. Combined with the squishy texture of corn and capsicum this Mexican casserole is lovely.

Mexican Black Bean Casserole

MAKES 6 X 1 CUP SERVES

1 tablespoon oil

1½ cups onion finely diced (around 1 onion)

2 cloves garlic finely chopped or crushed

1 cup red capsicum (bell pepper) finely diced (around 1)

1 small chilli de-seeded and finely chopped (optional)

1 tablespoon smoked paprika

400g (12oz) tin chopped tomatoes

2 x 400g (12oz) tins black beans drained

1½ cups frozen corn (or tinned)

1 teaspoon salt

1 tablespoon honey or date puree

½ cup cashew nuts

¾ cup water

garnish: Italian parsley

garnish: finely diced orange and red peppers

1. In a pot or pan saute the oil, onion, garlic, capsicum and chilli for 5 minutes or until the onion is soft.

2. Add the smoked paprika and stir for around 30 seconds to activate the flavours.

3. Add the tomatoes and one tin of the beans. Blend the mix with a stick blender.

4. Add the second tin of beans, corn, salt and honey and heat until it is just bubbling.

5. Blend the cashew nuts and water so it is a smooth cream. You may have to adjust the mixture a bit so you have a pourable cream that is not too runny.

6. Serve the beans with cashew cream on top and the colourful garnishes.

If you do not have a stick blender you can pour the mixture into a blender or food processor.

I love making a stir fry and adding other ingredients on top at the end. It looks great, saves dishes and is a complete meal. You can use any other protein like chickpeas or tofu instead of tempeh. Tempeh is a favourite and most people I make try it love it. So give it a go!

Quinoa Stir Fry with Tempeh

MAKES 8 X 1 CUP SERVES

½ cup quinoa

1 cup boiling water

250g (9oz) tempeh cubed

1 tablespoon oil

½ teaspoon salt

1½ cups onion finely diced (around 1 onion)

3 cups thickly chopped courgettes (zucchini) (around 3 medium)

3 cloves garlic finely chopped or crushed

1 tablespoon ginger puree or finely chopped

1 tablespoon oil

1 cup broccoli cut into small florets

10 stalks asparagus chopped

1 cup green peas frozen

½ teaspoon salt

1 cup cherry tomatoes cut in half

garnish: fresh coriander (cilantro)

1. In a pot combine the quinoa and boiling water and heat to bring back to the boil. Turn down to low and simmer with the lid on for 12 minutes or until the water has gone and the quinoa is soft. This should yield 1 cup of cooked quinoa.

2. In a pan saute the tempeh, oil and salt for around 10 minutes or until cooked and brown. Toss or stir regularly.

3. In a pot or pan saute the onion, courgettes, garlic, ginger and oil for around 5 minutes or until the onion is soft.

4. Add the broccoli, asparagus, green peas and salt and stir.

5. Add the cooked quinoa. Cook for another 5 minutes, stirring regularly.

6. Scatter the chopped tempeh and tomatoes on top. Garnish with fresh coriander.

Cherry Tomatoes

These little tomatoes look fantastic and are easy to prepare. I love mixing red and yellow tomatoes for more contrast and colour.

One evening I felt like mushrooms for dinner. I started sauteing them with a little garlic and thought they deserved to be better than just basic mushrooms. So I began adding some different ingredients and before long I had created this amazing combination. It is kind of a stir fry, but with mushrooms as the main event.

Hot Mushroom Mingle

MAKES 6X 1 CUP SERVES

2 teaspoons oil

150g (5oz) small button mushrooms (around 15)

1½ cups onion finely diced (around 1 onion)

2 cloves garlic finely chopped or crushed

1 tablespoon ginger puree or finely chopped

1 cup red capsicum (bell pepper) finely diced (around 1)

1 cup yellow capsicum (bell pepper) finely diced (around 1)

1 cup soy beans

100g (3oz) kale

½ teaspoon salt

2 tablespoons tahini

1 tablespoon sesame seeds

1. In a pot or pan saute the oil, mushrooms, onion, garlic and ginger for 5 minutes or until the onion is soft.

2. Add other vegetables and salt and cook for another 5 minutes or until everything is soft.

3. Serve garnished with a drizzle of tahini and sesame seeds.

Tahini varies in liquidity. If your tahini is not pourable just mix it with a little water to form a pourable version.

The key with this dish is cooking the mushrooms so they are tender, but not overcooked that they lose their volume.

You may have noticed that I love Thai food in my cookbooks and cafes. It just has a lovely blend of flavours. So here is a lovely stir fry that can be used as a meal on rice or as a very exciting side dish.

Thai Vegetable Stir Fry

MAKES 5 X 1 CUP SERVES

2 teaspoons oil

½ cup red onion diced (around ½ small onion)

1 tablespoon ginger puree or finely chopped

3 cloves garlic finely chopped or crushed

2 tablespoons diced lemongrass (fresh or frozen)

½ cup carrot julienne (around 1 medium carrot)

1 cup green beans

½ cup red capsicum (bell pepper) julienne (around ½)

½ cup yellow capsicum (bell pepper) julienne (around ½)

400g (12oz) tin baby corn

200g (6oz) tin bamboo shoots fine

1 tablespoon honey or date puree

1 teaspoon red Thai curry paste

2 tablespoons soy sauce or tamari

1 teaspoon arrowroot or 2 teaspoons cornflour

1 cup cold water

garnish: bean sprouts

garnish: coriander (cilantro)

garnish: cashew nuts

1. In a pot or pan saute the oil, onion, ginger, garlic, lemongrass and carrot for 5 minutes or until the onion is soft.

2. Add the beans and capsicum and cook for a further 3 minutes.

3. Add the corn, bamboo, honey, Thai curry paste and soy sauce and heat until just bubbling.

4. Mix the arrowroot with the cold water and pour in. Keep heating and it will thicken up.

5. Serve garnished with bean sprouts, coriander and cashews.

Another quick and easy meal using tofu and Thai curry paste.

Thai Green Curry Tofu

MAKES 4 X 1 CUP SERVES

650g (20oz) tofu frozen and defrosted

1½ cups onion finely diced (around 1 onion)

¼ cup coriander (cilantro) stalks finely chopped

1 tablespoon oil

1 tablespoon Thai green curry paste

1 cup red capsicum (bell pepper) roughly diced (around 1)

1 tablespoon honey or date puree

200ml (6oz) coconut cream

½ teaspoon salt

1 cup frozen green peas

garnish: fresh basil

1. Defrost the frozen tofu in some boiling water for around 10 minutes. Tear the tofu into chunks.

2. In a non-stick frying pan saute the tofu, onion, coriander stems and oil for 10 minutes or until the onion is soft.

3. Add the curry paste, capsicum and honey and continue to saute for another 5 minutes.

4. Add the remaining ingredients and warm until just bubbling.

5. Garnish with fresh basil or any other fresh herb.

Curry pastes are all different. Start off with a small amount and if it needs more flavour you can easily add more.

MAKES 7 X 1 CUP SERVES

½ cup long grain brown rice

1 cup boiling water

3 cups gold kumara (sweet potato) peeled and cubed (around 2 medium kumara)

1 tablespoon oil

1½ cups onion finely diced (around 1 onion)

1 cup red capsicum (bell pepper) finely diced (around 1 capsicum)

2 cloves garlic crushed or finely chopped

1 tablespoon finely chopped ginger or ginger puree

1 tablespoon oil

1 tablespoon yellow curry paste

1 tablespoon coriander

¼ cup hot water

¾ teaspoon salt

2 cups peas frozen

2 cups broad beans (fava beans) frozen

400g (12oz) tin black eyed beans

garnish: fresh coriander (cilantro)

This is a lovely Thai stir fry combination. The special bit is the lovely roasted kumara on top which makes it amazing. It is also fantastic served with hummus on top!

Thai Kumara Stir Fry

1. In a pot combine the rice and boiling water and bring to the boil. Cover and simmer on low heat for around 25 minutes or until the water has disappeared and the rice is soft and fluffy. This should yield 1½ cups of cooked rice.

2. Combine the kumara and oil and put on an oven tray. Bake at 180°C (350°F) for around 20 minutes or until the kumara is soft.

3. In a pot or pan saute the onion, capsicum, garlic, ginger and oil for around 5 minutes or until the onion is soft.

4. In a cup mix the curry paste and coriander with the hot water. Add to the curry.

5. Add the rest of the ingredients and heat for around 5 minutes while stirring, until all ingredients are heated and cooked through.

6. Serve with the cooked kumara on top.

7. Add a garnish of fresh coriander.

Every curry paste is different so add more if you need some more flavour.

Broad (Fava) Beans

When I was growing up these seemed to be in everyone's vegetable gardens. They are usually found in the freezer section of your supermarket. They defrost quickly under hot water or by heating in a dish. They have a lovely fresh taste. Use them in stir fries and salads.

I love it how most supermarkets now stock more than just one token style of brown rice. I try to make sure most of my ingredients are relatively easily available so when they pop up in my local supermarket that is often a sign they can appear in my cookbooks. Wild rice is great and adds excellent colour and crunch. Watch that you cook it properly as you do not want the rice too chewy or you can put people off eating rice forever.

Satay Wild Rice Risotto

MAKES 8 X 1 CUP SERVES

3 cups orange kumara (sweet potato) chopped into 2cm (1in) cubes

2 teaspoons oil

¾ cup wild rice mix

1½ cups boiling water

1 cup red onion roughly diced (around 1 small onion)

1 tablespoon ginger puree or finely chopped

3 cloves garlic finely chopped or crushed

200g (6oz) large button mushrooms halved (around 3 cups)

1 cup red capsicum (bell pepper) thinly sliced (around 1)

1 tablespoon oil

200g green beans (around 2 cups) fresh or frozen

3 tablespoons peanut butter

6 tablespoons hot water

1 tablespoon honey or date puree

1 teaspoon salt

¼ cup raw peanuts

garnish: coriander (cilantro)

1. In a pot combine the wild rice and boiling water and heat to bring back to the boil. Turn down to low and simmer with the lid on for 25 minutes or until the water has gone and the rice is soft. This should yield 2-3 cups of cooked rice.

2. In a bowl mix the kumara and oil together. Put onto an oven tray and bake at 180°C (350°F) for around 25 minutes or until just getting soft.

3. In a pot or pan saute the oil, onion, ginger, garlic, mushrooms and capsicum for 5 minutes or until the onion and mushrooms are soft.

4. Add the beans and cook for a further 3 minutes.

5. In a cup mix the peanut butter and hot water into a cream and add to the vegetables. Add the honey, salt and raw peanuts.

6. Stir in the cooked rice and kumara. Garnish with coriander.

Wild Rice Mix

These mixtures of rice are available at most supermarkets now. They generally contain red, black and brown rice. They are called many different names. Just make sure your mix is not just white rice with a few colourful grains tossed in.

Amaranth is a fantastic grain that I keep in my cupboard and occasionally have for breakfast. In the past I had found it difficult to make practical savoury recipes with it. So I tried this dish which is kind of like a stir fry and it tastes great.

Amaranth & Root Vege Mingle

MAKES 5 X 1 CUP SERVES

2 cups carrots diced 1cm (½in) (around 2 carrots)

2 cups parsnip diced 1cm (½in) (around 2 parsnip)

2 teaspoons oil (bake)

½ cup amaranth

1 cup boiling water

2 teaspoons oil (saute)

1½ cups onion finely diced (around 1 onion)

3 cloves garlic finely chopped or crushed

1 tablespoon ginger puree or finely chopped

2 cups broad beans (fava beans) (usually bought frozen)

2 tablespoons soy sauce or tamari

garnish: ¼ cup fresh coriander (cilantro) finely sliced

garnish: 1 teaspoon finely sliced fresh red chilli

1. In a bowl mix the carrots, parsnips and oil together. Put onto an oven tray and bake at 180°C (350°F) for around 30 minutes or until just getting soft.

2. In a pot combine the amaranth and boiling water and heat to bring back to the boil. Turn down to low and simmer with the lid on for 20 minutes or until the water has gone and the amaranth has a consistency like porridge. This should yield 1 cup of cooked amaranth.

3. In a pot or pan saute the oil, onion, garlic, ginger and broad beans for 5 minutes or until the onion is soft.

4. Add the roast vegetable mix and amaranth to the pan. Stir and heat gently until everything is hot. Add the soy sauce.

5. Serve garnished with coriander and chilli.

The broad beans will defrost quickly so you do not need to pre-cook.

If the amaranth is gluggy stir in a little more water to make it easy to mix.

Amaranth

Amaranth is a super food grain. It is great as a porridge for breakfast or you can use it in a stir fry like this recipe. It acts kind of like oats in that it goes fairly mushy and sticks together. Although it can take 20 minutes to cook.

Main Meals

Gado Gado 76

Mini Pumpkin Frittatas 78

Mega Bean Tacos 80

Indian Sweet Potato Rosti 82

Tuscan Wholemeal Pizza 84

Indian Spinach & Potato Wrap 86

Carrot & Beet Fritters 88

Bramboracky (Czech Pancake) 90

Butternut Mac Cheese 92

Chunky Italian Tomato Pasta 94

Green Vegetable Cakes 96

Mexican Bean Enchilada 98

This is a popular Indonesian salad with peanut sauce and usually served with chicken. This peanut sauce is very quick and does not require cooking.

Gado Gado

MAKES 8 X 1 CUP SERVES

2 cups potatoes chopped into 1cm (½in) cubes

TOFU:

350g (10oz) firm tofu cubed

2 teaspoons oil

½ teaspoon salt

GADO GADO SAUCE (MAKES AROUND 1 CUP)

2 cloves garlic

2 tablespoons honey or date puree

1 cup roasted peanuts (or ¾ cup peanut butter)

1 tablespoon lime juice

1 teaspoon sesame oil

¼ cup water

1 tablespoon soy sauce or tamari

optional: 1 teaspoon tamarind paste

ADDITIONS

1 cup green beans

1 cup cherry tomatoes quartered

1 cup cucumber diced

1 cup red cabbage thinly sliced

1 cup mung bean sprouts

garnish: fresh coriander (cilantro)

1. Put the potatoes into a pot with boiling water and cook for 15 minutes or until they are soft.

2. In a pot or pan saute the tofu, oil and salt for around 10 minutes or until the tofu is browned.

3. Put the sauce ingredients into a blender and blend until you have a smooth sauce.

4. Prepare the additions and put into a bowl.

5. Serve with the warm tofu and potato and drizzle the sauce over the top.

6. Garnish with freshly chopped coriander.

7. Mix just before you serve.

You can serve on the table in one big dish like the photo, or you can portion out into individual bowls so everyone can mix their own plate.

This dish relies on the tofu and potato being hot. You may like to heat the sauce in a pot before serving if all the ingredients are cold.

Believe it or not - a frittata without eggs! Give it a go you will be surprised how good it is!

Mini Pumpkin Frittatas

MAKES 8 FRITTATAS

3 cups pumpkin or butternut squash chopped into 2cm (1in) cubes

2 teaspoons oil (for oven)

2 teaspoons oil (for saute)

1 cup red onion sliced (around 1 small onion)

1 cup red capsicum (bell pepper) roughly diced (around 1)

¼ cup chickpea (besan) flour

350g (10oz) firm tofu

1 teaspoon salt

½ teaspoon turmeric

1 tablespoon arrowroot

2 cloves garlic

up to ¼ cup water

garnish: chopped parsley

1. In a bowl mix the pumpkin and oil together. Put onto an oven tray and bake at 180°C (350°F) for around 15 minutes or until just getting soft.

2. In a pot or pan saute the oil, onion and capsicum for 5 minutes or until the onion is soft.

3. Put the chickpea flour, tofu, salt, turmeric, arrowroot and garlic into a blender and blend until you have a smooth batter that is pourable. You may have to add extra water and continue to blend.

4. Line each hole in a large muffin tin with baking paper. Put the pumpkin and onion mixture in the trays. You want this to almost fill the trays.

5. Pour the batter mixture over the vegetables. Tap the tray on your counter to make sure it fills in all the spaces. You may need to use a knife to gently stir the contents to ensure there are no air gaps.

6. Put in the oven and bake at 180°C (360°F) for 20 minutes or until the frittatas are set but still soft.

7. Serve garnished with parsley.

This is tacos with a difference. The Thai curry paste will add a dimension of flavour that goes very well with this colourful Mexican meal. And you will love the healthy tahini dressing.

Mega Bean Tacos

MAKES 6 TACOS

1½ cups onion finely diced (around 1 onion)

2 cloves garlic finely chopped or crushed

1 cup red capsicum (bell pepper) roughly diced (around 1)

1 teaspoon Thai red curry paste

2 teaspoons oil

1 tablespoon honey or date puree

½ teaspoon salt

½ of a 400g (12oz) tin chopped tomatoes

400g (12oz) tin red kidney beans (drained)

6 tacos

tahini dressing (page 141)

SALAD VEGETABLES:

mesclun lettuce

tomato diced

yellow capsicum (bell pepper) diced

avocado diced

1. In a pot or pan saute the onion, garlic, capsicum, curry paste and oil for around 5 minutes or until the onion is soft.

2. Add the honey, salt, tomatoes and kidney beans.

3. Half blend the mixture. You can use a stick blender to blend half the mixture. Or put half the mixture into a food processor or blender and blend.

4. Pre-heat the tacos briefly in the oven if desired.

5. Add the bean filling and vegetables.

6. Drizzle some tahini dressing over the top.

Tacos can be messy to eat. The best way is to use your hands!

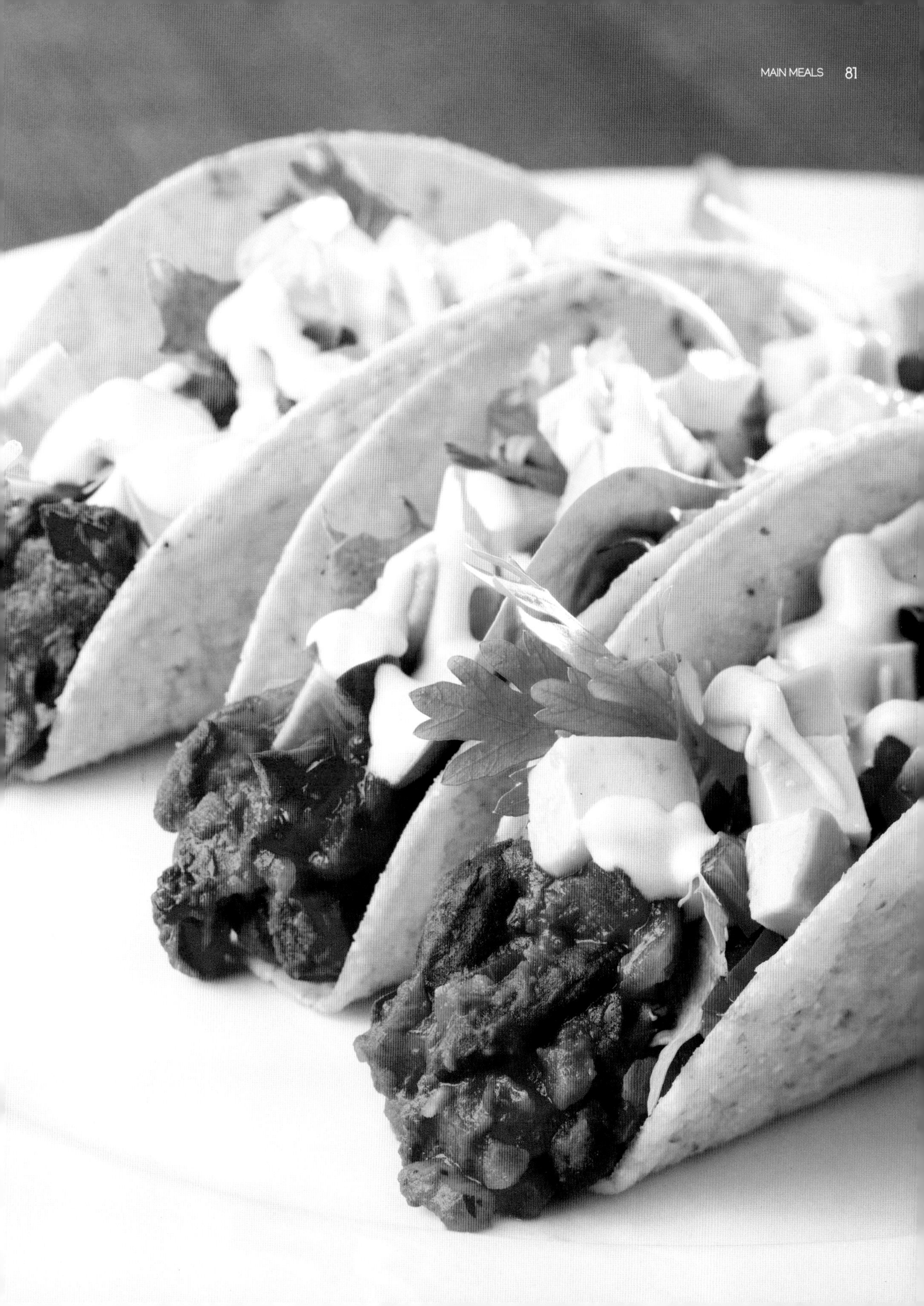

At my local supermarket there is a similar product that is sold pre-made in the freezer. It looks delicious except that it contains heaps of oil and flavour enhancers. So I thought I would make some home-made ones that taste great without all of the nasties. Also the cost of homemade meals like this is usually 20% of the cost of purchasing pre-made.

Indian Sweet Potato Rosti

MAKES 16 SMALL ROSTI

4 cups red kumara (sweet potato) cubed (around 1 large kumara)

1 cup red onion diced (around 1 small onion)

1 cup red capsicum (bell pepper) roughly diced (around 1)

3 cloves garlic finely chopped or crushed

2 teaspoons oil

½ cup frozen peas

½ cup frozen spinach

½ teaspoon turmeric

1 tablespoon ground coriander

1 teaspoon salt

oil for shallow frying

sesame seeds

1. Cook the cubed kumara in a pot of boiling water for 15 minutes or until soft. Drain and mash roughly.

2. In a pot or pan saute the onion, capsicum, garlic and oil for around 5 minutes or until the onion is soft.

3. Add the peas and spinach and cook for a further 5 minutes.

4. Add the spices and salt and cook for around 30 seconds to activate the flavours.

5. Combine the onion mix with the mashed kumara. Do not over mix - you want to retain some of the chunky bits.

6. Put a dash of oil into a non-stick frying pan. Form the mixture into 3 tablespoon balls with your hands and squash down. Fry for around 2 minutes each side.

7. Before putting the rosti in the pan sprinkle some sesame seeds in the pan.

8. Serve with fresh greens and sweet chilli sauce.

Make sure you use red kumara as the other varieties (gold, orange) have a different consistency when cooked which will make the rosti go mushy and they will not hold together.

This is my first exploration into baking bread. With this pizza you will only need 1 or 2 slices to feel full as there is so much more fibre compared to white pizza bases.

Tuscan Wholemeal Pizza

MAKES 8 SLICES

BASE

8g (¼oz) pack bakers yeast

1 cup warm water

1 teaspoon sugar

2 cups wholemeal flour

½ teaspoon salt

1 tablespoon oil

extra wholemeal flour

TOPPINGS

2 cups pumpkin or butternut squash chopped into 1cm (½in) cubes

2 teaspoons oil

3 cups Italian tomato sauce (page 138)

1 cup kalamata olives pitted

1 cup cherry tomatoes halved

GARNISH

parmeshew cheese (page 137)

fresh baby rocket (rucola)

1. In a bowl mix the pumpkin and oil together. Put onto an oven tray and bake at 180°C (350°F) for around 15 minutes or until just getting soft.

2. Put the yeast, warm water and sugar into a bowl. Let it sit for 5 minutes.

3. In a larger bowl mix together the flour, salt and oil. Make a well in the centre and pour in the yeast mix. Mix it all together so you have a dough. You may have to add a little more flour to achieve the right texture. Knead it for around 5 minutes.

4. Put a little oil into a mixing bowl and put the dough in it. Roll it around so it is coated. Put some cling wrap on top of the bowl and keep in a warm place for 1 hour or until it has doubled in size.

5. Put some flour on your bench and put the dough on the bench and fold it around several times, punching it. Press it out so you have a round pizza base around 5mm (⅙in) thick. Put it on an oven tray or better still a pizza stone.

6. Spread the tomato sauce on top and add the toppings.

7. Bake at 200°C (400°F) for 12 minutes or until the base is cooked.

8. Garnish with the parmeshew cheese and baby rocket.

This is the only time in all my books where normal sugar is used. This is necessary to activate the yeast to make the dough.

I am not normally a wrap person, however there are only 3 words to describe this dish: Yum, Yum and Yum! Backed up by my recipe tester Nyree who scored it 5 out of 5.

Indian Spinach & Potato Wrap

MAKES 5 WRAPS

4 cups potato chopped into 2cm (1in) cubes

2 teaspoons oil

1 cup red onion sliced (around 1 small onion)

2 cloves garlic finely chopped or crushed

1 tablespoon oil

350g (10oz) firm tofu cubed

½ teaspoon salt

½ teaspoon turmeric

200g baby spinach (around 4 cups pressed down)

1 cup red capsicum (bell pepper) roughly diced (around 1)

5 wholemeal wraps

1. In a bowl mix the potato and oil together. Put onto an oven tray and bake at 180°C (350°F) for around 20 minutes or until just getting soft.

2. In a pot or pan saute the onion, garlic and oil for around 5 minutes or until the onion is soft.

3. Add the tofu to the pan and cook for around 10 minutes or until the tofu is firming up. Sprinkle over the turmeric and salt.

4. Stir in the roasted potato, spinach and capsicum and cook for another 3 minutes or until the spinach is wilted.

5. Put 1 cup of the mixture in the middle of the wrap, spread out and roll tightly. Repeat for all the wraps.

6. Cut in half and serve.

Optional: Spray with a little oil and put under the grill (broiler) for around 2 minutes to crispen the wraps up. You can also put in a sandwich press.

Make sure you cut the ingredients as small as you can which makes it easier to wrap and eat.

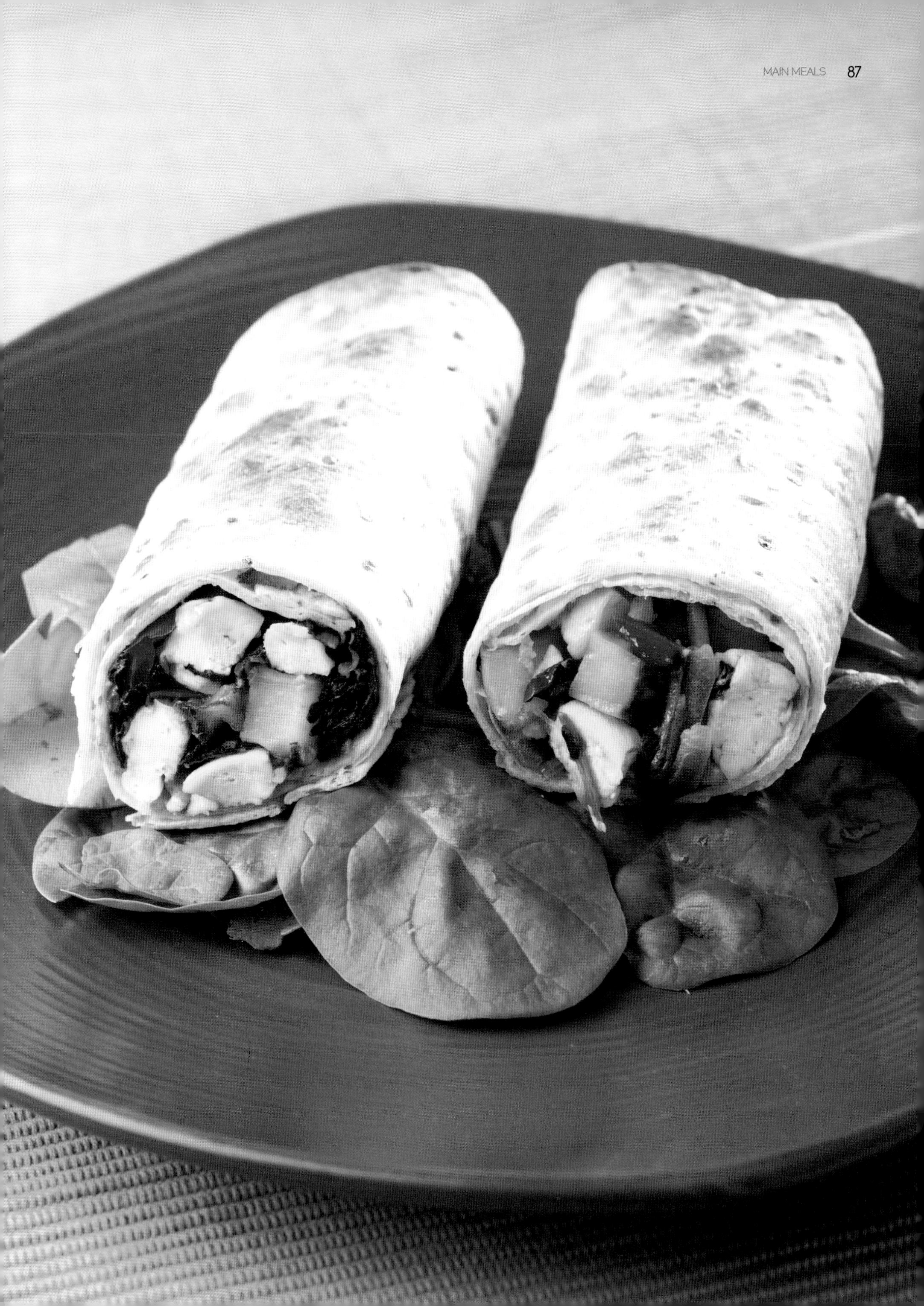

I ran a cooking demonstration followed by a "team cook" session where contestants had to create a version of my dish, and I judged the result. The teams had to create a fritter - for example carrot, corn or courgette. The carrot team decided to add some beetroot to their mix and it ended up tasting great. I was originally going to just make carrot fritters for this recipe but added some beetroot and it is great! This recipe cooks the ingredients first, but you can omit this step and go for a more raw and earthy flavour.

Carrot & Beet Fritters

MAKES 10 FRITTERS

1½ cups onion finely diced (around 1 onion)

1 clove garlic finely chopped or crushed

1 cup carrot grated (around 1 large carrot)

1 cup beetroot grated (around 1 medium beetroot)

1 tablespoon oil

2 teaspoons cumin ground

1 cup chickpea (besan) flour

2 tablespoons sweet chilli sauce

¾ cup chopped mint

1 teaspoon salt

up to ¾ cup water

oil for shallow frying

1. In a non-stick frying pan saute the onion, garlic, carrot, beetroot and oil for 5 minutes or until the onion is soft.

2. Put the onion mixture into a mixing bowl and add all remaining ingredients (except water and oil). Mix well. Add enough water so you have a mixture that is pourable but not runny.

3. Add a little oil to the same pan.

4. Shallow fry for around 2 minutes each side or until there is a crust forming.

5. Let sit on a paper towel while you are cooking them all.

6. Serve on a bed of cherry tomatoes and baby spinach, with a dollop of hummus on top.

I always make a test fritter when starting and adjust the mixture and/or pan temperature for the rest.

Believe it or not, the beautiful blue dish used for this photo is actually a glazed pot plant dish I found in a hardware store.

My wife's cousin Lydia told us to head to some markets in Christchurch as there was a stall there with amazing potato pancakes run by a couple from the Czech Republic. I looked everywhere but could not find them and then found out they had recently retired. Lydia explained them to me and here is a healthy version which I hope you enjoy. Often potato pancakes or fritters require you to use raw potatoes which in turn requires a huge amount of oil to cook them. This method allows you to cook them with minimal amounts of oil.

Bramboracky (Czech Pancake)

MAKES 18 PANCAKES

2 teaspoons oil

750g (24oz) potatoes (around 2 large)

1½ cups onion finely diced (around 1 onion)

2 cloves garlic finely chopped or crushed

1 tablespoon caraway seeds

1 cup chickpea (besan) flour

¾ cup milk of your choice

1 teaspoon salt

oil for shallow frying

SERVE WITH:

sauerkraut

fried button mushrooms

garnish: Italian parsley

1. Halve the potatoes. Put in a pot with boiling water and cook for around 20 minutes or until they are 75% cooked. You want them to be soft while retaining some strength. Put them in a bowl of cold water to cool them down. Using a hand grater, grate the potato.

2. In a pot or pan saute the oil, onion, garlic and caraway seeds for 5 minutes or until the onion is soft.

3. Combine the grated potatoes, onion mix and remaining ingredients in a bowl and mix well.

4. Add a little oil to a hot non-stick frying pan, and put ¼ cup scoops of the potato mixture into the pan. Cook for around 2 minutes per side.

5. Serve with sauerkraut, fried mushrooms and garnish with Italian parsley.

I always do one pancake as a test to start with. I can then adjust the heat, or make the mixture more runny (add more milk) or thicker (add more flour).

This dish would also be great with some aioli, hummus or tahini dressing.

This is a New Zealand classic dish. By now you probably realise I am going to ditch some of the ingredients - white flour pasta, cheese and milk are not the best products to eat for a meal. This healthier version uses wholemeal pasta (which you can find at most supermarkets these days) and a healthy cashew cheese. But to make it even more delicious the sauce is made with butternut pumpkin which gives it fantastic flavour.

Butternut Mac Cheese

MAKES 8 X 1 CUP SERVES

250g (8oz) wholemeal or rice penne pasta (or any variety with a hole through the middle)

SAUCE:

3 cups butternut pumpkin cubed (around 1 small butternut)

2 teaspoons oil

2 cups milk (soy, rice, oat or almond)

½ teaspoon salt

1 teaspoon dijon mustard

½ cup raw cashew nuts

2 tablespoons nutritional yeast flakes

½ cup red capsicum (bell pepper) finely diced (around ½ capsicum)

TOPPING:

3 tablespoons cashew nuts

1 tablespoon nutritional yeast flakes

garnish: parsley chopped

1. Cook the pasta in boiling water as per the packet directions. This is usually around 8-10 minutes. Drain well.

2. In a bowl mix the pumpkin and oil together. Put onto an oven tray and bake at 180°C (350°F) for 20 minutes or until just getting soft.

3. Put the topping ingredients (cashew nuts and yeast flakes) into a blender or food processor and blend until you have a bread crumb like texture. Set aside in a separate bowl.

4. Put the pumpkin, milk, salt, mustard, cashews and yeast into a blender or food processor and blend until smooth. You may have to add a little more milk to get a pourable mixture.

5. In a bowl combine the pumpkin sauce, red capsicum and the pasta well. Pour into a flat serving dish.

6. Sprinkle the topping mixture on top. You can also spray the top lightly with an oil spray.

7. Put into the oven and fan bake at 180°C (400°F) for 15 minutes or until the top starts going crunchy and golden.

8. Garnish with chopped parsley and serve.

The sauce will thicken when cooked so make it runnier than you think you will need it to be.

Make sure you blend the topping ingredients first, that way you do not have to clean the blender inbetween.

You can buy good pasta sauces in the supermarket which is good when you do not have time. However preparing a great Italian tomato sauce is so easy once you have done it once and the taste is amazing (and much better for you). Give this recipe a go and you will never buy supermarket sauces again!

Chunky Italian Tomato Pasta

MAKES 6 X 1 CUP SERVES

250g (8oz) penne corn pasta (or your favourite pasta)

½ cup red onion diced (around 1 small onion)

1½ cups onion finely diced (around 1 onion)

6 cloves garlic finely chopped or crushed

1 tablespoon mixed herbs

1 tablespoon oil

2 tablespoons honey or date puree

2 x 400g (12oz) tins chopped tomatoes

4 tablespoons tomato paste

1 teaspoon salt

garnish: chopped basil and Italian parsley

1. Cook the pasta as per the packet directions or until al dente (firm to the bite). This is usually for 8 minutes in boiling water. Drain well immediately.

2. In a pot or pan saute the onion, garlic, herbs and oil for around 5 minutes or until the onion is soft.

3. Add the remaining ingredients.

If this dish is the main part of your meal you could add some protein to it like canned beans, chickpeas or some diced tofu.

Corn Pasta

Most pasta in supermarkets is made with heavily processed white flour. Try some of the corn varieties which are gluten free and easier to digest. There are also some good wholemeal varieties and some made with grains like rice and quinoa. Cook to the packet directions.

I saw some really green cakes in a cafe once and thought it would be nice to do some fritters that were jam packed with green stuff. So here are the results of that experimentation.

Green Vegetable Cakes

MAKES 15

1 tablespoon oil

1 cup courgette (zucchini) finely diced (around 1 courgette)

1 cup frozen peas

½ cup red onion finely diced

1 cup spinach frozen

1 cup chickpea (besan) flour

½ teaspoon salt

½ cup water

¼ cup coriander (cilantro) chopped

2 tablespoons sesame seeds

oil for shallow frying

1. In a pot or pan saute the oil, courgette, peas, onion and spinach for 5 minutes or until the onion is clear.

2. In a bowl add the chickpea flour and water and mix until it is a thick paste.

3. Add the coriander, sesame seeds and hot vegetable mix and combine. You may need to add a little water to make a thick but pourable batter.

4. Form into patties and shallow fry with a little oil for around 2 minutes per side.

5. Serve with Tzatziki (page 136).

Chop the vegetables really small so the patties form easily.

Annelise, one of my recipe testers, said that all 3 of her children and her husband absolutely loved this recipe (which apparently does not happen that often). So you can chalk this up as a kid friendly meal.

MAKES 6 ENCHILADAS

3 cups Italian tomato sauce (page 138)

400g (12oz) tin red kidney beans

¼ teaspoon salt

1 cup red onion thinly sliced (around 1)

2 cloves garlic crushed or finely chopped

1 cup red capsicum (bell pepper) thinly sliced (around 1)

1 cup yellow capsicum (bell pepper) thinly sliced (around 1)

1 cup orange capsicum (bell pepper) thinly sliced (around 1)

1 teaspoon oil

6 wholemeal tortillas

garnish: parmeshew cheese (page 137)

garnish: parsley

Mexican Bean Enchilada

1. Make the tomato sauce.

2. In a pot or pan, heat the beans and salt.

3. In a pot or pan saute the onion, garlic, capsicum and oil for around 5 minutes or until the onion is soft.

4. Spoon the beans and capsicum mix into the centre of the tortilla and roll up. Repeat for all the enchiladas.

5. Put in a lightly oiled baking dish. Cover with the tomato sauce.

6. Bake at 180°C (350°F) for around 5 minutes or until heated through.

7. Garnish with parmeshew cheese and parsley.

Soups

Hearty Dark Legume Soup 102

Mexican Green Pepper Soup 104

Roast Vege Soup with Dukkah 106

Tom Yum Soup 108

Old School Vegetable Soup 110

Chunky Chickpea Soup 112

This is a lovely soup for a cold winter's night.

Hearty Dark Legume Soup

MAKES 6 X 1 CUP SERVES

1½ cups onion finely diced (around 1 onion)

3 cloves garlic finely chopped or crushed

1 tablespoon oil

1 tablespoon smoked paprika

1 cup brown (crimson) lentils

6 cups boiling water

400g (12oz) tin black beans

1 tablespoon honey or date puree

1 teaspoon salt

2 tablespoons tamari or soy sauce

garnish: chives sliced thinly

garnish: cashew cream (page 140)

1. In a pot or pan saute the onion, garlic and oil for 5 minutes or until the onion is clear.

2. Add the smoked paprika and stir for 30 seconds to activate the flavours.

3. Add the lentils and water. Bring back to the boil and simmer for 30 minutes or until the lentils are soft.

4. Add the remaining ingredients.

5. Serve garnished with chives and cashew cream.

I once had an enchilada in a Mexican restaurant and it came with a delicious green sauce over the top. I thought the sauce would make a great soup by leaving out the cheese. As a result I created this lovely capsicum and coriander soup with an amazing unique flavour.

Mexican Green Pepper Soup

MAKES 4 X 1 CUP SERVES

2 teaspoons oil

1½ cups onion finely diced (around 1 onion)

3 cloves garlic finely chopped or crushed

3 cups green capsicum (bell pepper) roughly diced (around 3)

1 cup fresh coriander (cilantro) roughly chopped, including stalks

½ cup cashew nuts

2 cups water

¾ teaspoon salt

garnish: tortilla strips

garnish: fresh coriander (cilantro)

1. In a pot saute the oil, onion, garlic, capsicum and coriander for 15 minutes or until the capsicum is soft.

2. Put the cashew nuts and 1 cup of water in a blender and blend until you have a cashew milk. Add to the pot along with the remaining cup of water.

3. Heat until it is nearly boiling.

4. Add the salt and blend with a stick blender until you have a smooth texture.

5. Serve with some toasted tortilla strips and a garnish of fresh coriander.

Green Capsicum

I usually do not use green capsicum (bell pepper) as they are less sweet than other colours. But when I do I always cook them really well and do not usually use them raw (except as a garnish).

I had a similar soup in an airline lounge once and it was very tasty, except it was very watery and the dukkah was lost in the soup. I much prefer thick soups so here is my upgraded version! It is a great experience when you take a mouthful of the lovely soup, the creamy cashew cream, and the crunchy dukkah!

Roast Vege Soup with Dukkah

MAKES 10 X 1 CUP SERVES

6 cups vegetables finely diced

- parsnip

- pumpkin (butternut)

- orange kumara (sweet potato)

- eggplant (aubergine)

- carrot

1 tablespoon cumin

1 tablespoon coriander

1 tablespoon oil

1½ cups onion finely diced (around 1 onion)

4 cloves garlic finely chopped or crushed

2 teaspoons oil

4 tablespoons tomato paste

2 x 400g (12oz) tins chopped tomatoes

1 teaspoon salt

1 tablespoon honey or date puree

2 cups boiling water

½ cup cashew nuts

¾ cup cold water

garnish: Turkish dukkah (page 140)

garnish: Italian parsley chopped

1. Cut the vegetables into small cubes. In a bowl mix the vegetables, spices and oil together. Put onto an oven tray and bake at 180°C (350°F) for around 30 minutes or until just getting soft.

2. In a pot or pan saute the onion, garlic and oil for around 5 minutes or until the onion is soft.

3. Add the tomato paste, chopped tomatoes, salt, honey and boiling water and bring back to the boil.

4. Stir in the roasted vegetables.

5. Put the cashew nuts and water in a blender and blend until they are a smooth cream.

6. Serve the soup with cashew cream, dukkah and some chopped Italian parsley.

This is a great dish that Thai restaurants often have on the menu as a starter. It is a flavoursome soup but often contains fish and oyster sauce. Here is my version with none of these things and it still tastes great!

Tom Yum Soup

MAKES 10 X 1 CUP SERVES

6 cups boiling water

2 tablespoons tom yum curry paste

3 tablespoons finely chopped lemongrass

6 kaffir lime leaves (optional)

1 carrot julienne

1 large tomato diced

1 red onion diced

7 button mushrooms quartered

1 cup red capsicum (bell pepper) roughly diced (around 1)

300g (10 oz) firm tofu diced 1cm (½in)

3 tablespoons soy sauce

3 tablespoons honey or date puree

½ teaspoon salt

garnish: fresh coriander

garnish: fresh kaffir lime leaves

garnish: lime juice

1. Combine all the ingredients in a pot.

2. Simmer for 30 minutes.

3. Taste and adjust with more curry paste, soy sauce and/or honey as required.

4. Garnish and serve.

You can use a red Thai curry paste if you cannot find tom yum.

MAKES 8 X 1 CUP SERVES

2 teaspoons oil

1½ cups onion finely diced
(around 1 onion)

3 cloves garlic finely
chopped or crushed

1 cup carrot diced (around
1 large carrot)

1½ cups celery diced
(around 2 stalks)

1½ cups courgettes
(zucchini) chopped (around
2 medium)

1 cup red capsicum (bell
pepper) roughly diced
(around 1)

1 teaspoon Thai red
curry paste

12 cups boiling water

¾ cup pearl barley

½ cup French puy lentils

2 bay leaves

1 tablespoon honey or
date puree

3 tablespoons
tomato paste

1 teaspoon salt

garnish: chopped parsley

This is a lovely old-school style of vegetable soup using lentils and barley. The type your grandmother would have made. I have never used pearl barley much so was keen to try it out in this soup which is delicious and very warming.

Old School Vegetable Soup

1. In a pot or pan saute the oil, onion, garlic, carrot, celery, courgettes and capsicum for 5 minutes or until the onion is soft.

2. Add the curry paste and stir in. You may need to mix a little water to the curry paste so it spreads evenly.

3. Add the water, barley, lentils and bay leaves. Bring back to the boil.

4. Turn the heat down and simmer for 45 minutes or until the barley is soft.

5. Add the remaining ingredients.

6. You may need to add some more boiling water if it is too thick.

Pearl Barley

This is a lovely ingredient for soups and hotpots as it swells up, and is chewy. It is also a whole grain. You need to make sure you cook it properly until it is soft which can take up to 45 minutes.

This was a quick lunch one stormy Sunday afternoon after working on this cookbook. I used up some ingredients in the fridge and threw it together in minutes. I am not normally a fan of "watery" soups, however this was delicious! So I decided to include it in this cookbook at the last minute.

Chunky Chickpea Soup

MAKES 10 X 1 CUP SERVES

2 teaspoons oil

1½ cups onion finely diced (around 1 onion)

3 cloves garlic finely chopped or crushed

1½ cups celery diced (around 2 stalks)

1 cup red capsicum (bell pepper) roughly diced (around 1)

1 cup orange capsicum (bell pepper) roughly diced (around 1)

1 teaspoon Thai red curry paste

1 teaspoon Thai green curry paste

8 cups boiling water

2 tablespoons honey or date puree

1 teaspoon salt

1 cup frozen peas

400g (12oz) tin of chickpeas (garbanzo beans)

garnish: chopped parsley

1. In a pot or pan saute the oil, onion, garlic, celery, and capsicum for 10 minutes or until the onion is soft.

2. Add the curry paste and stir in. You may need to mix a little water with the curry paste to help it spread evenly.

3. Add the boiling water, honey, date puree and salt.

4. Bring back to the boil and then turn down to a simmer for around 5 minutes to let the flavours mingle.

5. Just before serving add the peas and chickpeas.

6. Garnish with chopped parsley.

Every curry paste is different so check the flavour, saltiness, sweetness and hotness and adjust if necessary.

You can use your favourite curry paste for this recipe if you do not have green and red.

Sides

Colcannon 118

Rainbow Vegetables 120

Bruschetta 121

Chunky Penang Thai Tofu 122

Bubble & Squeak 124

Sweet Potato Hash 126

Tomato & Zucchini Mingle 127

We were eating mashed potato one night when Dawn, a friend of ours, suggested this Welsh version of mashed potatoes. There seems to be many varieties of this recipe - usually with lashings of butter and/or cheese through it. But this version tastes great and is an excellent accompaniment to any meal.

Colcannon

MAKES 8 X 1 CUP SERVES

6 cups potatoes roughly diced (around 6 medium) unpeeled

1 tablespoon oil

1 large leek sliced

2 cloves garlic finely chopped or crushed

1 cup frozen spinach

3 cups savoy cabbage finely sliced

2 tablespoons dijon mustard

1 teaspoon salt

1 cup milk of your choice

1 spring onion (scallion) finely sliced

garnish: parsley

1. Put the potatoes in a pot of boiling water. Bring back to the boil, and simmer for 15 minutes or until soft. Drain and then mash roughly.

2. In a pot or pan saute the oil, leeks, garlic, spinach and cabbage for 8 minutes or until the mixture is soft.

3. Combine the potatoes, vegetable mix and remaining ingredients and mix gently.

4. Serve garnished with parsley.

The spring onions make this a very fresh dish. If you do not like the raw onion taste you can put them in earlier with the leeks and cook them.

If you have leftovers you can form into patties, coat with some wholemeal bread crumbs and fry in a little oil.

Savoy Cabbage

I call this "wrinkly" cabbage. It gives a really nice texture to any dish and can be used anywhere white cabbage is usually used. Try it next time you are cooking cabbage or making a coleslaw.

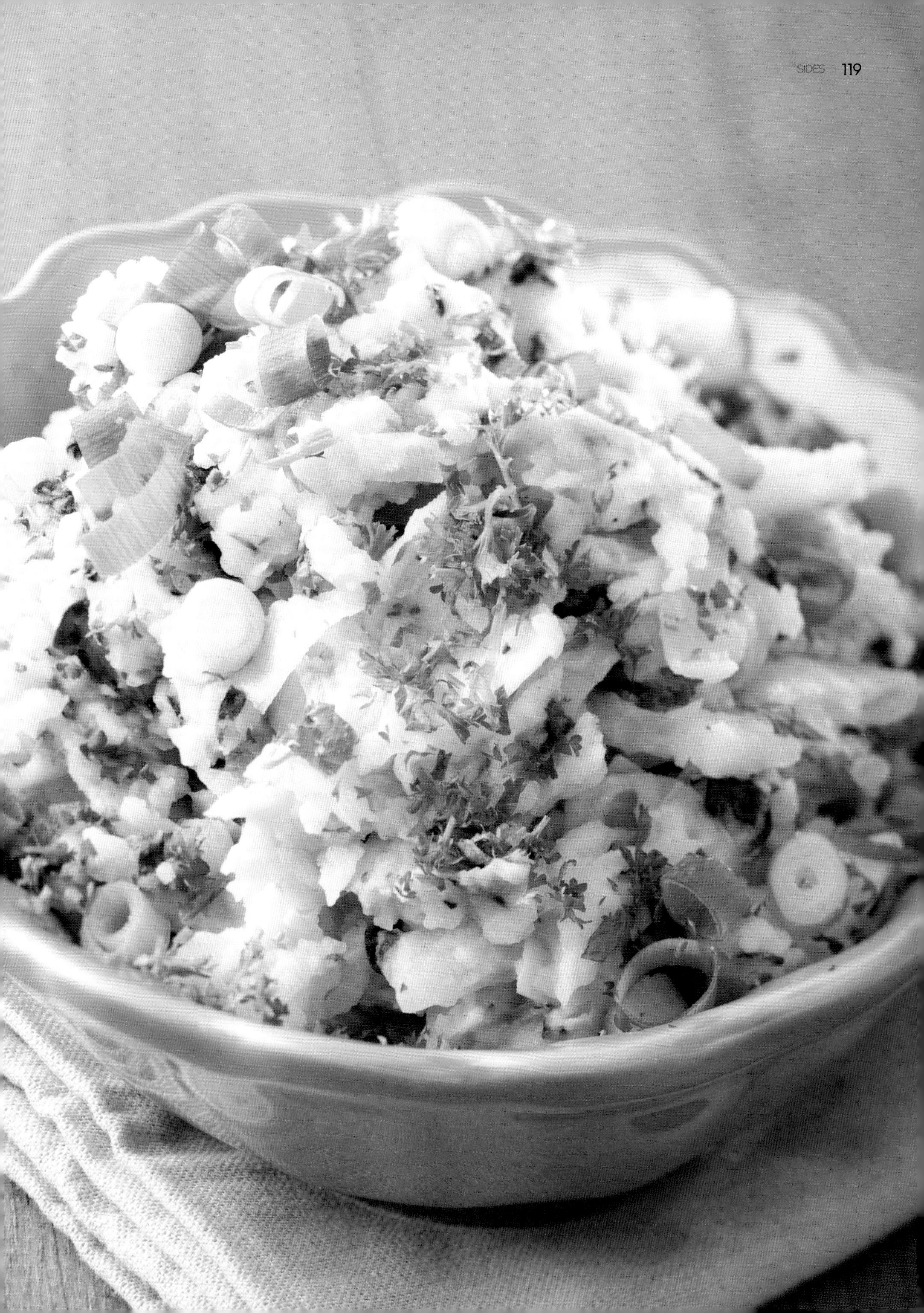

This is a lovely stir fry I developed for a breakfast to go with scrambled tofu.

Rainbow Vegetables

MAKES 4 X 1 CUP SERVES

1 tablespoon oil

10 button mushrooms sliced

1 cup red onion thinly sliced (around 1 medium onion)

2 cups courgettes (zucchini) halved and sliced (around 2 medium)

1 cup red capsicum (bell pepper) thinly sliced (around 1)

1 cup yellow capsicum (bell pepper) thinly sliced (around 1)

1 teaspoon salt

100g baby spinach

garnish: Italian parsley

1. In a pot or pan saute the oil, mushrooms and onion for 5 minutes.

2. Add the other vegetables and salt and cook for another 5 minutes until they are just soft. Stir regularly.

3. Garnish with Italian parsley.

This is a great Italian favourite that you will usually find served up with diagonally sliced French bread sticks made from white flour. It works just as well on some healthier whole grain bread! Give it a try - it is a great appetiser or light lunch snack!

Bruschetta

MAKES 12

3 large slices whole-grain bread

3 teaspoons olive oil

1½ cups cherry tomatoes (mixed colours if possible)

1 clove garlic finely chopped or crushed

10 basil leaves

¼ tablespoon salt

1. Put bread on an oven tray and brush with olive oil. Grill (broil) in the top of the oven for around 2 minutes or until slightly brown. Cut into quarters.

2. Cut the tomatoes, garlic and basil leaves as small as you can and mix together with the garlic and salt.

3. Put the tomato mixture on the top of the hot bread pieces and serve immediately.

MAKES 5 X 1 CUP SERVES

600g (18oz) firm tofu

1 tablespoon oil

2 cloves garlic finely chopped or crushed

1 tablespoon oil

½ cup carrot finely sliced (around 1 medium carrot)

½ cup red capsicum (bell pepper) finely sliced (around ½)

½ cup yellow capsicum (bell pepper) finely sliced (around ½)

1 teaspoon Penang Thai curry paste

4 tablespoons water

1 tablespoon honey or date puree

½ teaspoon salt

2 tablespoons soy sauce or tamari

garnish: 1 tablespoon sesame seeds black

garnish: 1 tablespoon sesame seeds white

garnish: chopped fresh coriander (cilantro)

Despite tofu having a bad reputation for being bland and boring, I love it. It soaks up flavours really well. A really quick way to use it is to add some Thai curry paste. This version makes an interesting side dish and could almost be a meal if served on brown rice!

Chunky Penang Thai Tofu

1. Cut the tofu into large 2cm (1in) chunks.

2. In a non-stick frying pan, saute the tofu and oil for around 10 minutes or until firming up. Stir or toss regularly.

3. In another pot or pan, saute the garlic, oil, carrot, capsicum for 5 minutes or until soft.

4. In a cup, combine the curry paste with the water, honey, salt and soy sauce and stir well. Pour over the tofu and let it soak up all the flavours.

5. Add the vegetable mix to the tofu and mix well.

6. Serve with freshly chopped coriander on top.

Be gentle when stirring the tofu as it can easily break apart.

Tamari

Tamari is like soy sauce except it does not usually have wheat in it. It often has a slightly richer yet less salty flavour. Give it a try! You can use Tamari and soy sauce interchangeably. It is available at many supermarkets and most health and whole foods stores.

I started out making some kumara rosti and realised I had the wrong coloured kumara as it was falling apart and not sticking together like a fritter should. The mix was wrong for rosti but the flavour was delicious. So I mashed it up some more, made a few additions and here it is a delicious bubble and squeak. This is a great chefs technique; when a dish is not working out or is very different to the plan, just change the name and no one will notice!

Bubble & Squeak

MAKES 4 X 1 CUP SERVES

4 cups orange kumara (sweet potato) diced un-peeled

1 cup red onion diced (around 1 small onion)

3 cloves garlic finely chopped or crushed

2 teaspoons oil

2 teaspoons cumin

1 cup frozen peas

1 cup frozen spinach

1 teaspoon salt

garnish: sesame seeds

garnish: fresh coriander (cilantro)

1. Put the kumara into a pot covered with boiling water and bring back to the boil. Simmer for around 10 minutes or until the kumara is soft. Drain the water and mash roughly.

2. In a pot or pan saute the onion, garlic and oil for around 5 minutes or until the onion is soft.

3. Add the cumin and stir in for around 30 seconds to activate the flavours.

4. Add the peas, spinach, salt and mashed kumara and mix together.

5. Continue cooking for another 3 minutes to ensure the peas defrost.

6. Serve garnished with sesame seeds and coriander.

You can use fresh spinach for this recipe although you will need around 4 cups packed.

This delicious mingle is a very tasty side dish that can also be used at a hot breakfast!

Sweet Potato Hash

MAKES 5 X 1 CUP SERVES

2 cups potato diced 1cm (½in) (around 1 large potato)

4 cups orange kumara (sweet potato) diced 1cm (½in)

1 tablespoon oil

1 cup red onion sliced (around 1 small onion)

3 cloves garlic finely chopped or crushed

¾ teaspoons salt

garnish: parsley

1. Put the chopped potato, kumara (sweet potato) and boiling water in a pot, bring back to the boil and simmer for 20 minutes or until soft. Drain.

2. In a pot or pan saute the oil, onion and garlic for around 5 minutes or until the onion is soft.

3. Add the potato and kumara (sweet potato) to the onion mix and cook (stirring regularly) for 5 minutes. Stir in the salt.

4. Garnish with finely chopped parsley.

I sometimes put the cooked potato on a chopping board and chop them randomly to roughen them up and make the dish more rustic.

Tomatoes and zucchini go together really well and work
fantastically with the parmeshew cheese!

Tomato & Zucchini Mingle

MAKES 5 X 1 CUP SERVES

1 tablespoon oil

2 cups courgettes (zucchini)
thickly siced (around 2)

2 cloves garlic finely
chopped or crushed

2 cups tomatoes
roughly chopped

1 tablespoon honey or
date puree

¼ teaspoon salt

garnish: parmeshew cheese
(page 137)

garnish: Italiian parsley

1. In a pot or pan saute the oil, courgettes and garlic for 5 minutes or until the
   courgettes are soft.

2. Add the tomato, honey and salt and cook for another 3 minutes,
   mixing gently.

3. Drain off any excess liquid.

4. Serve garnished with parmeshew cheese and Italian parsley.

You can use drained tinned whole tomatoes if fresh tomatoes are out
of season.

Flavour Boosters

Carrot & Coriander Dip 130

Green Pea Dip 132

Buttery Spread 133

Kalamata Olive Dressing 134

Indonesian Peanut Dip 135

Tzatziki 136

Parmeshew Cheese Sprinkle 137

Revive Aioli 138

Italian Tomato Sauce 138

Basil Pesto 139

Date Puree 139

Turkish Dukkah 140

Cashew Cream 140

Classic Hummus 141

Tahini Dressing 141

I found a similar product in the dips section of our supermarket and it was great. I checked the ingredients and it had quite a bit of oil and preservatives. So here is a redeveloped healthy version of an amazing dip you will love! Make sure you try freshly toasted pita strips to go with it!

Carrot & Coriander Dip

MAKES 2½ CUPS

8 cups diced carrot (around 4 large)

1 tablespoon coriander

1 tablespoon oil

3 tablespoons tahini

2 tablespoons lemon juice

1 clove garlic

½ cup water

garnish: coriander (cilantro)

garnish: olive oil

serve with: wholemeal pita

1. In a bowl mix the carrots, coriander and oil together. Put onto an oven tray and bake at 180°C (350°F) for 20 minutes or until just getting soft.

2. Put the cooked carrots and remaining ingredients into a blender and blend until smooth.

3. Garnish with some fresh coriander and a drizzle of olive oil. Serve with wholemeal pita bread or dippers of your choice.

Wholemeal Pita Strips

A delicious addition to any platter or with dips. Slice pita into strips and lightly spray with oil. Bake in a low oven for 5 minutes, or until warm and crispy. Make sure you get wholemeal!

This is so easy to make and is delicious. Nice when you want something a little different to hummus.

Green Pea Dip

MAKES 6 CUPS

400g (12oz) tin chickpeas (garbanzo beans) drained (around 2 cups)

4 cups frozen green peas defrosted (reserve 2 cups until the end)

1 teaspoon salt

2 tablespoons tahini

4 tablespoons lemon juice

½ cup water

3 cloves garlic peeled

optional: handful of mint

1. Put all ingredients in a food processor except 2 cups of the green peas.

2. Process until fine. You may need to add a little more water to achieve the desired consistency.

3. Put in the remaining 2 cups of green peas and process for a couple of seconds so there are pieces of green peas (but there are no whole peas). This adds interest and texture to the dip.

4. Serve with corn chips, rice crackers or vegetable dippers.

To defrost the frozen green peas simply put them in some hot water for a couple of minutes.

This is a lovely neutral spread that is a great dairy-free option. Agar agar is a healthy gelatin alternative usually found in Asian supermarkets.

Buttery Spread

MAKES 1½ CUPS

¼ cup hulled millet

¾ cup boiling water

1½ teaspoons agar agar

¾ cup cold water

½ cup cashew nuts

½ teaspoon salt

⅛ teaspoon turmeric

1. In a pot combine the millet and boiling water and heat to bring back to the boil. Turn down to low and simmer with the lid on for 15 minutes or until the water has gone and the millet is soft. This should yield ¾ cup of cooked millet.

2. In a small pot or frying pan combine the agar agar and cold water and heat. Cook for around 5 minutes or until it has been bubbling for around 1 minute.

3. Put the cooked millet, agar agar mixture and remaining ingredients into a blender and process until smooth.

4. Put in a storage container and refrigerate.

This will keep in the fridge for around 2-3 days.

If the texture is too stodgy add a little more water and re-blend.

A tangy dressing that can turn an average salad into a fantastic one and is great as a dip or as an additional flavour drizzled on a main. Your guests will be asking you for the recipe!

Kalamata Olive Dressing

MAKES 1 CUP

1 cup kalamata olives pitted

1 clove garlic

1 tablespoon honey or date puree

4 tablespoons tahini

2 tablespoons lemon juice

2 tablespoons water

1. Put all ingredients into a blender and blend.

If your olives are not overly salty you may wish to add a little salt to this dressing.

This was an experimental gado gado sauce that ended up being too thick. I dipped some crackers in and it was amazing so it became a dip recipe!

Indonesian Peanut Dip

MAKES AROUND 2 CUPS

2 cloves garlic

1 tablespoon honey or date puree

1 cup roasted peanuts (or ¾ cup peanut butter)

1 tablespoon lime juice

1 teaspoon sesame oil

¼ cup water

1 tablespoon soy sauce or tamari

400g (12oz) tin red kidney beans

extra water: up to ½ cup

1. Put all ingredients into a blender and blend until smooth. You may need to add some extra water.

This is an excellent dip to serve with meals like fritters or even use as a dip with crackers and vegetable sticks. Usually this recipe combines yoghurt with the cucumber.

Tzatziki

MAKES 2 CUPS

½ cup cashew nuts

½ cup sunflower seeds

½ cup water

3 tablespoons lemon juice

2 cloves garlic

1 teaspoon salt

¼ cup mint chopped

1 cup finely chopped cucumber

1. Put the cashew nuts, seeds, water, lemon juice and garlic in a blender. Blend for 30 seconds or until it is smooth. If the blender stalls you may need to push down the ingredients or add a little more water.

2. Chop the cucumber longways into strips, and then across these so you have long matchsticks. Slice them thinly so you end up with very finely diced cucumber.

3. Mix the salt with the cucumber and let sit a couple of minutes for the salt to draw out the moisture. Drain off the liquid and use a paper towel to remove as much moisture as you can.

4. Add the cucumber and mint to the cream and mix well.

This is a fantastic healthy way to substitute parmesan cheese!!! I accidently discovered it when I was making the Butternut Mac Cheese recipe (page 92) and wanted something for the topping.

Parmeshew Cheese Sprinkle

MAKES ½ CUP

½ cup roasted cashew nuts

1 tablespoon nutritional yeast flakes

1. Put the ingredients into a blender and blend for around 30 - 60 seconds until you get a bread crumb type texture. The time will depend on your blender.

2. You may have to use a spoon to take the mixture off the sides of the blender and re-blend to get it consistent.

Don't worry if there are small cashew pieces in the mix - this keeps it interesting.

The recipe will also work with raw cashew nuts if you do not have roasted.

Store this in a sealed container in the refrigerator.

Revive Aioli

MAKES 3 CUPS

½ cup soy milk

1 tablespoon cider vinegar or lemon juice

3 cloves garlic

1 tablespoon whole grain mustard

½ teaspoon salt

2 cups oil

½ to 1 cup room temperature water

1. Select a blender, food processor or stick blender.

2. Blend all ingredients (except oil and water).

3. While blending, slowly add oil and then add water at end until desired consistency is reached.

When making dressings you need to ensure that all items are at room temperature, and that you add the oil slowly.

Aioli will last 2-3 weeks in your refrigerator.

Italian Tomato Sauce

MAKES 6 CUPS

1½ cups onion chopped (around 1 onion)

4 cloves garlic crushed

2 tablespoons oil

3 x 400g (12oz) tins tomatoes

¾ teaspoon salt

1 teaspoon mixed dried herbs

3 tablespoons honey or date puree

1. In a pot saute onion, garlic and oil until clear.

2. Add remaining ingredients and cook until bubbling.

3. Blend all the sauce with a stick blender.

If you really like garlic add twice as much for a great garlic taste.

Basil Pesto

MAKES 2 CUPS

1 large bunch fresh basil (around 125g/4oz)

½ cup oil

1 cup cashew nuts raw

½ teaspoon salt

¼ cup lemon juice (around 2 lemons)

2 cloves garlic

1. Put all ingredients into a food processor and blend until it is well mixed, but there are still some nut pieces showing.

2. You can use a blender or stick blender but you will have to add a little more oil or water to make the mixture turn.

For a different flavour you can use almonds or walnuts instead of cashew nuts.

Traditionally pesto uses pine nuts - however these are around 4 times the price of almonds and cashews.

Use coriander (cilantro) instead of basil for a different pesto.

Date Puree

MAKES 2 CUPS

2 cups pitted dried dates

2 cups boiling water

1. Put dates in boiling water for 5 minutes to soften.

2. Put the water and dates in blender and blend well until you have a smooth paste.

3. If you hear date stones (as they occasionally come through), sieve the puree.

4. Put into an air-tight container and store in the refrigerator.

You can use cold water to soak the dates - however it will take several hours for them to soften.

Date puree will last 2-3 weeks in your refrigerator.

THE RECIPES ON THESE PAGES HAVE BEEN REPEATED FROM "THE REVIVE CAFE COOKBOOKS 1 & 2"

Turkish Dukkah

MAKES 1 CUP

1 tablespoon oil

1 cup almonds and/or cashew nuts

1 tablespoon cumin seeds

2 tablespoons coriander seeds

½ tablespoon fennel seeds

1 tablespoon sesame seeds

1. Put all ingredients onto an oven tray and bake at 180°C (350°F) for 5 minutes.

2. Let the mixture cool slightly.

3. Place in a food processor and blend very briefly until slightly blended but not into dust. You want a mixture of nut dust and uneven pieces.

4. This will keep for many weeks in a sealed, air-tight container in the refrigerator.

Cashew Cream

MAKES 1½ CUPS

1 cup cashew nuts raw

½ cup water

optional: 2 tablespoons honey or date puree

optional: 1 drop of vanilla essence

1. Put all ingredients into a blender or use a stick blender.

2. Blend well until smooth.

3. You may need to add more water to achieve the consistency you are after.

The cream is very nice with just water and cashew nuts, however add the vanilla and honey if you want a sweet version.

To make this amazing, add a tin of pears (with juice) instead of the water and you have cashew and pear cream.

Classic Hummus

MAKES 3 CUPS

2 x 400g (12oz) cans of chickpeas (garbanzo beans)

½ teaspoon of salt

2 cloves of garlic chopped or crushed

2 tablespoons tahini (ground hulled sesame seed paste)

½ cup water

4 tablespoons lemon juice

1. Put all ingredients in food processor and blend until smooth. You can also use a stick blender or a regular blender however you may have to add more water to keep it flowing.

2. Taste. Note that all batches vary in flavour as salt, chickpeas and lemon juice always have different flavours and consistency.

3. Add extra water/salt/lemon juice as needed. You should be able to taste every ingredient slightly, with not too much of any ingredient coming through.

My previous recipes have had oil in hummus - however I now just replace with water.

Tahini Dressing

MAKES 1 CUP

4 tablespoons tahini

4 tablespoons lemon juice

½ teaspoon salt

1 large clove garlic

1 tablespoon honey or date puree

4 tablespoons water

1. Put all ingredients into a blender and blend until smooth.

2. Or for a quick method put all ingredients except garlic into a small bowl and stir well until creamy.

Using honey will give a white dressing, while date puree will make this dressing a light brown colour.

THE RECIPES ON THESE PAGES HAVE BEEN REPEATED FROM "THE REVIVE CAFE COOKBOOKS 1 & 4"

Breakfasts

Supercharged Breakfast Bowl 144

Oat Waffles with Wild Berries 146

Amazing Thai Scrambled Tofu 148

Blueberry Power Breakfast Shake 150

Feijoa Buckwheat Pancakes 152

Homemade Natural Muesli 154

Naked Strawberry Jam 156

Super Quick Rice Breakfast 158

SERVES 4

HONEY GINGER TOFU

600g (20oz) tofu cut into very tiny cubes

2 teaspoons oil

¼ teaspoon turmeric

1 tablespoon ginger puree

¼ teaspoon salt

1 tablespoon honey

BEANS

1 tin (2 cups) black beans

1 tablespoon soy sauce or tamari

SWEET POTATO O'BRIEN

3 cups red kumara (sweet potato) chopped small (around 2 medium kumara)

½ teaspoon salt

1 cup red capsicum (bell pepper) chopped (around 1 capsicum)

1 cup red onion finely chopped (around 1 small onion)

2 teaspoons oil

TOMATO

2 cups cherry tomatoes

½ teaspoon oil

pinch salt

garnish: avocado

garnish: fresh coriander

garnish: lime wedges

My wife Verity attended a seminar with lovely plant based food and came back raving about the awesome hot breakfast she had there with black beans, tofu and potatoes. I decided to see if I could replicate it. I did not have all the ingredients required but created this amazing combination. I asked her if it was the same - she said "not quite, but it is delicious all the same!"

Supercharged Breakfast Bowl

1. In a hot pot or pan saute the honey ginger tofu ingredients for around 15 minutes or until starting to go brown. Stir regularly.

2. Put the beans and soy sauce into a pot or pan and heat.

3. In a bowl mix the sweet potato O'Brien ingredients together. Put onto an oven tray and bake at 180°C (350°F) for around 15 minutes or until just getting soft.

4. Put the tomato ingredients into a small pan and heat for about 2 minutes or until they are warm and starting to get soft.

5. Serve in bowls with a garnish of avocado, fresh coriander and lime wedges.

You could also add some hummus or chutney to this mix.

Many waffle recipes and the packet mixes are loaded with white flour, artificial additives and sugar. So I combined many different healthy recipes together and finally came up with this one. It actually worked and did not stick in the waffle maker like so many other mixtures do.

Oat Waffles with Wild Berries

MAKES 6 WAFFLES

2 tablespoons ground flaxseed (flax meal)

4 tablespoons boiling water

2 cups rolled oats

½ cup cashew nuts

½ teaspoon salt

2¼ cups water

1 tablespoon oil

2 tablespoons honey or date puree

oil spray

TOPPING SUGGESTIONS

cashew cream

honey or maple syrup

fresh or frozen berries

banana

1. In a cup combine the flaxseed and boiling water and let sit for 5 minutes. This will make a flaxseed gel that is a great binding agent.

2. Put the oats, cashew nuts, salt, water, oil, honey and flaxseed gel into a blender and blend until smooth.

3. Spray your waffle maker with oil and put the mixture in as per the waffle iron directions. For my waffle maker I put in ½ cup of mixture for 4 minutes.

4. Put on a plate and smother with toppings of your choice.

You can also add ½ cup cornmeal (polenta) to help make them crispy.

Flaxseed Gel

This is a great binding agent you can use instead of eggs. Just soak 1 tablespoon of ground flaxseeds (linseeds) in 2 tablespoons of boiling water for 5 minutes and it forms a gel. Mix this in with any baking or item requiring binding. It can only really be used for binding so will not make an omelette!

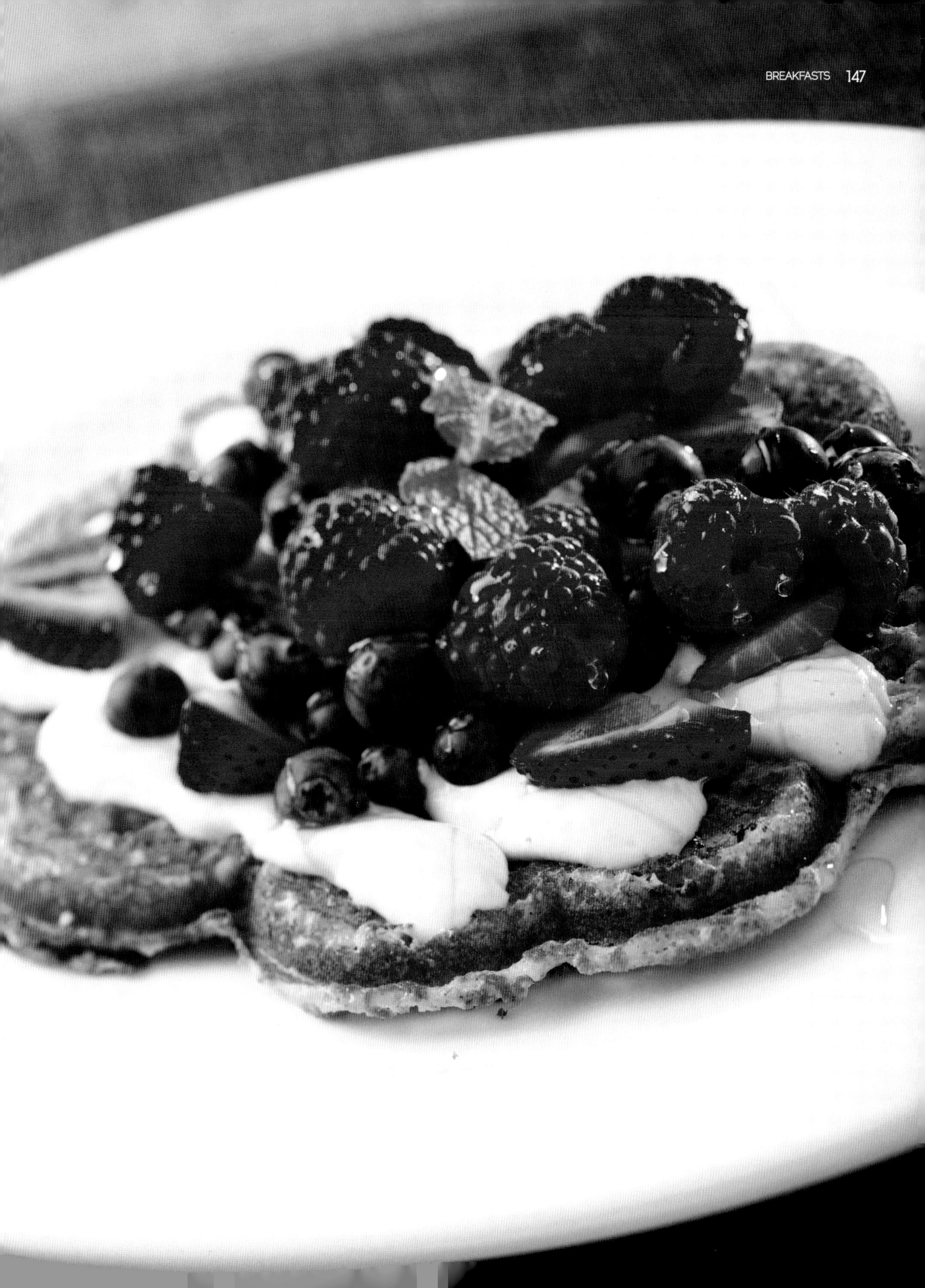

I was home working on my cookbooks on a rainy day and decided to have scrambled tofu on toast for lunch. It got me thinking how I have never ever flavoured scrambled tofu with Thai flavours. So I tried it and it worked well. I also did not have any coriander so used mint instead and it created an amazing flavour. I already have a scrambled tofu recipe in my first cookbook so was not planning on including this, however it tastes so amazing I could not hide it from the world!

Amazing Thai Scrambled Tofu

MAKES 4 X 1 CUP SERVES

½ cup red onion finely chopped (around ½ red onion)

2 cloves garlic finely chopped or crushed

1 cup courgette (zucchini) randomly chopped (around 1 large courgette)

1 tablespoon oil

300g (10oz) firm tofu crumbled

1 tablespoon tamari or soy sauce

1 tablespoon Thai Penang curry paste

½ teaspoon salt

1 tablespoon honey or date puree

2 tablespoons lime juice (around 1 lime)

¼ cup mint sliced (around 1 large stalk)

serve with:
whole grain toast

garnish: extra mint

1. In a pot or pan saute the onion, garlic, courgette and oil for 5 minutes or until the onion and courgette are soft.

2. Add the tofu and continue to saute for another 5 minutes or until the tofu is browning.

3. Add the tamari, curry paste, salt and honey and mix in well.

4. Just before serving stir in the mint and lime juice.

5. Serve on whole grain toast.

If the courgettes are releasing too much moisture just turn up the heat and cook until it evaporates.

Curry pastes are all different so stir in some more if you need more flavour.

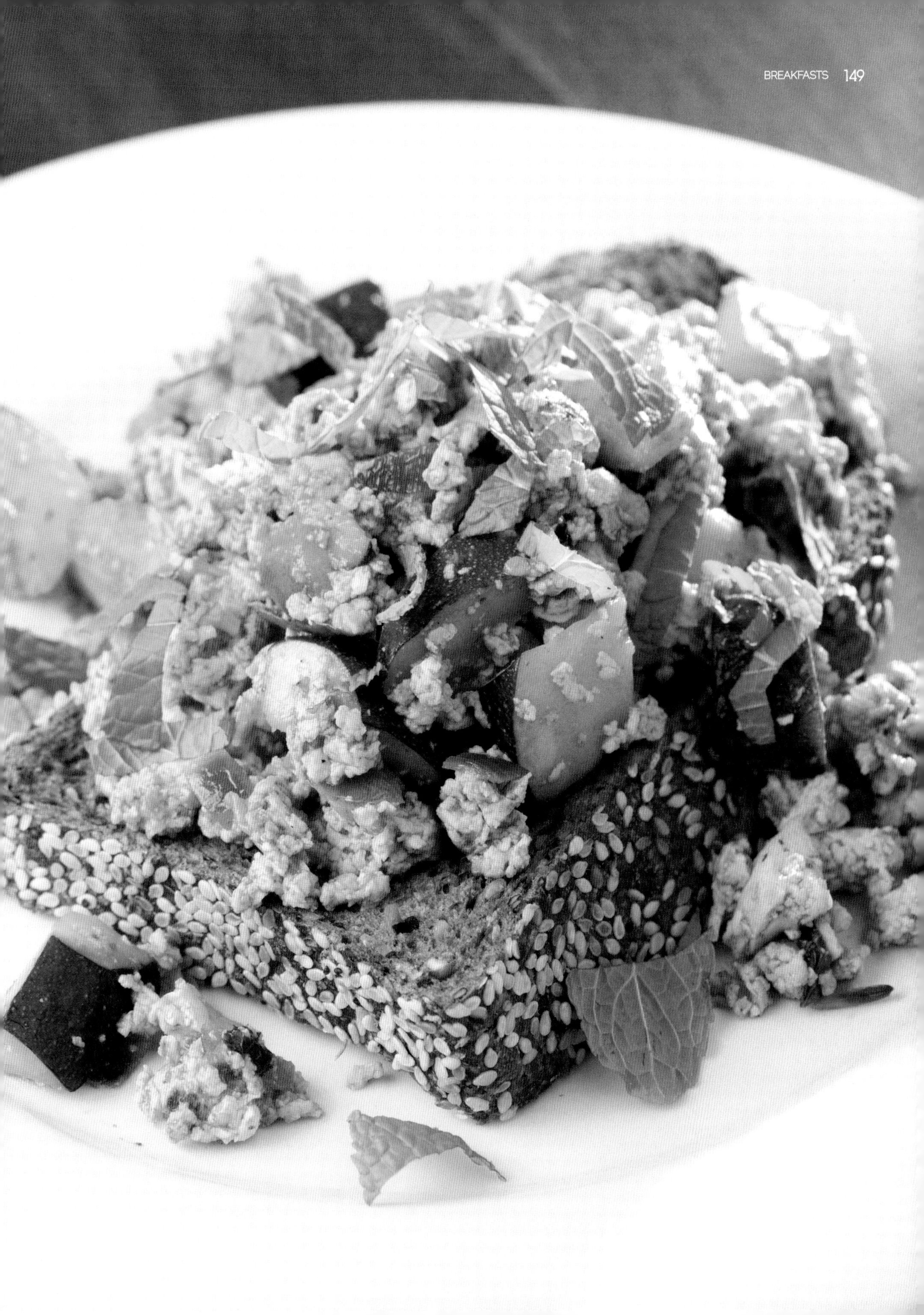

This is an amazing way to start your day. Protein, good fats, grains, fruit and a lot of excellent stuff. The chia seeds and flax meal gel up and make this smoothie thick and creamy.

Blueberry Power Breakfast Shake

MAKES 2 X 1 CUP SERVES

1 cup milk of your choice

1 large banana

1 cup frozen blueberries

1 tablespoon flax meal
(ground linseeds)

1 tablespoon chia seeds

½ avocado

½ cup cooked quinoa

garnish: blueberries

garnish: chia seeds

garnish: mint leaves

1. Put all ingredients into a blender and blend.

2. Pour into glasses and garnish.

Always put the softer ingredients in the bottom of the blender when making smoothies. That way the blender is up to speed when the harder ingredients start hitting the blade and they are introduced slowly.

If you want a striped look add a couple of tablespoons of milk to the blender at the end and blend for around 1 second. When you pour into a glass you will have streaks of un-mixed milk.

Instead of quinoa you could use brown rice, oats or any other whole grain you have leftover in the fridge.

My wife Verity requested I make these. Firstly because she is gluten-free and loves pancakes, secondly, she loves feijoa. The flax gel and coconut flour helps to keep these guys sticking together. The feijoa adds little bursts of flavour.

Feijoa Buckwheat Pancakes

MAKES 12

2 tablespoons flaxseed ground

¼ cup boiling water

1 cup buckwheat flour

2 tablespoons coconut flour

1 teaspoon baking powder

⅛ teaspoon salt

1 cup water

1 cup milk of your choice

2 tablespoons honey or date puree

6 feijoas (pineapple guavas) scooped out and finely chopped (yielding 1 cup)

oil for shallow frying

garnish: maple syrup

garnish: sesame seeds

garnish: extra feijoa sliced

1. In a cup mix the ground flaxseed and water and leave to sit. After a couple of minutes it will form a gel.

2. In a bowl mix the flours, baking powder and salt. Pour in the water and mix. Pour in the milk and honey and mix into a batter.

3. Add the flax gel and mix well. Let sit for 5 minutes and mix again.

4. Add the feijoa.

5. Heat a good non-stick frying pan with a bit of oil.

6. Put in around 2-3 tablespoons of batter in the pan and cook for around 1 minute per side.

7. Serve with some finely chopped feijoa strips, sesame seeds and maple syrup on top.

You can substitute other fruit in this recipe. Grated apple and kiwifruit are good.

This recipe is also great for making plate-sized pancakes too.

Coconut Flour

A great flour used for thickening things especially in baking. Use sparingly as you will need less than you think. It really sucks up moisture.

Whenever we travel to Christchurch to stay with my parents (or my wife's parents) we are always treated to homemade muesli! Everyone has their own ideas of what muesli should be like. My mother-in-law enjoys a more toasted muesli. While this recipe is similar to my mum's - a natural muesli with raw rolled oats mixed with some fruit and nuts. The best way to start the day!

Homemade Natural Muesli

MAKES 15 X ½ CUP SERVES

½ cup Brazil nuts
roughly chopped

½ cup pumpkin seeds

½ cup almonds sliced

½ cup cashew pieces

½ cup shredded coconut

½ cup sesame seeds

½ cup dried cranberries

½ cup dried apricot diced

4 cups rolled oats (oatmeal)
fine cut

SERVE WITH:

fresh fruit

milk of your choice

1. Put the Brazil nuts, pumpkin seeds, almonds and cashew pieces in a hot non-stick frying pan and heat for around 5 minutes or until the nuts are starting to turn brown. Shake the pan regularly. Pour into a mixing bowl.

2. Put the coconut and sesame seeds into the hot pan and heat for around 3 minutes or until the ingredients start to brown. Pour into the mixing bowl.

3. Add fruit and rolled oats to the mixing bowl and combine.

4. Let cool and store in a sealed jar or container.

5. Serve with fresh fruit and milk of your choice.

This recipe does not add sugar for sweetening so you may wish to drizzle a little honey on top when you serve it.

Dry Pan Roasting

Get a good non-stick frying pan and you can actually roast some items (particularly nuts and seeds) without oil. Just keep the pan moving and look out for any browning. This is much quicker than roasting in an oven.

Jams are usually packed with a huge amount of white sugar. Try this recipe for a healthy version. You can also make apricot, boysenberry, raspberry and blueberry jam the same way. It is also great for a dessert topping or on your healthy breakfast!

Naked Strawberry Jam

MAKES 3 CUPS

5 cups frozen strawberries

½ cup honey

1 teaspoon agar agar powder

3 teaspoons cold water

1. Put the frozen strawberries and honey in a pot and heat until the strawberries are soft.

2. Mix the agar agar and water in a cup and pour in.

3. Cook bubbling for a further 5 minutes.

4. Pour into your storage container. It will thicken when it cools.

This is not a long term preserving recipe. It needs to be kept in the fridge and used within 2 weeks.

This recipe is dependent on the amount of agar agar used. Too much and it will go very jelly like; too little and it may stay runny.

Agar Agar

Also called "Agar", it is a powder that often comes in little pouches and is inexpensive. It is a healthy alternative to gelatine and is made from algae (think seaweed). Generally you add it to a liquid sweet dish, bring it to the boil and let it set. You can also buy it in strips but this takes extra work. You can find agar in Asian grocery stores and some whole food stores.

This is one of my favourite quick breakfasts. Whenever I cook rice I always cook extra for such an occasion. Just throw some ingredients into a pot, grate an apple and the breakfast is virtually done. It contains all you need for a great start to your day. Change this recipe to whatever fruit is in season or whatever dried fruits and nuts you like best.

Super Quick Rice Breakfast

MAKES 2 X 1 CUP SERVES

1 cup cooked brown rice

½ cup milk of your choice

2 tablespoons almonds ground

2 tablespoons cranberries

¼ teaspoon clove powder (optional)

½ apple grated

garnish: ½ banana sliced

garnish: ¼ cup blueberries

garnish: 1 tablespoon sliced almonds

1. Put the rice, milk, ground almonds, cranberries and clove powder in a pot and warm up until hot (around 3 minutes).

2. Grate the apple and add to the pot and mix.

3. Serve in a bowl with bananas, blueberries and almonds on top.

Drizzle over a little honey if you like some extra sweetness.

Almond Meal

This is a great way to thicken up any dish and add creaminess. You can buy ground almond at some health stores. However I find it easier and fresher to grind my own using a coffee grinder. Just store in the refrigerator.

Sweet Things

Chia Seed Choc Pudding. 162

Homemade Lemonade Quencher. 164

Energiser Smoothie. 165

Cranberry Oatie Balls 166

Cucumber & Mint Ice Cream 168

Pineapple & Mint. 170

Strawberry Slushy. 171

Fruit Salad with Peach Cream 172

Vegg Nog 174

Everyone loves chocolate based puddings and this is a great healthy version using nuts, carob and dates instead of dairy, chocolate and sugar!

Chia Seed Choc Pudding

MAKES 2 X ¾ CUP SERVES

¼ cup dates

¼ cup cashews

3 tablespoons carob powder

1¼ cups water

¼ cup chia seeds

garnish: ¼ cup frozen raspberries

garnish: shredded coconut

1. Put the dates, cashews, carob and water in a blender and blend until you have a creamy milk.

2. Transfer to a bowl or jug. Add the chia seeds and mix quickly and well.

3. Put in the refrigerator for around 1-2 hours. The chia seeds will expand and this will thicken the pudding.

4. Stir and serve in glasses with a garnish of frozen raspberries and a sprinkle of shredded coconut.

Some chia seeds (often when they have been heat treated) do not swell up and produce a nice thick and creamy texture. If this recipes does not work it is most likely because of your chia seeds. If this is the case take them back to the shop you bought them from.

For an even creamier texture, use your favourite milk instead of water.

Chia Seeds

These little wonder-seeds not only have great nutritional properties, but provide a lovely creamy gel-like texture when mixed with liquids. Great for smoothies and desserts - give them a try! They take between 10 -30 minutes to swell up.

There is nothing like lemonade to quench your thirst on a hot day - the trouble is that any store-bought varieties contain heaps and heaps of processed sugar - which is not good for you and will destroy your immune system. So here is a better version which uses honey for sweetener.

Homemade Lemonade Quencher

MAKES 3 X 1 CUP SERVES

¼ cup boiling water

3 tablespoons honey

4 tablespoons lemon juice

500ml soda water or sparkling mineral water

ice

mint

lemon slices

1. In a cup mix the boiling water and honey until the honey has melted.

2. Add lemon juice.

3. Pour the lemon honey syrup into 2 glasses and then pour over the soda water.

4. Add ice, lemon slices and mint leaves.

This was one of our first smoothies when I started Revive in 2005. It is so refreshing and simple and a very popular option. Just 3 ingredients.

Energiser Smoothie

MAKES 2 X 1 CUP SERVES

2 oranges peeled

1 large banana

2 cups frozen strawberries

1. Put the orange and banana in the bottom of a blender, followed by the strawberries on top.

2. Blend until smooth.

This order is important as if you put the hard frozen strawberries at the bottom the blender may not get enough liquid generated to blend correctly.

Here is a lovely healthy sweet ball snack that is made from oats. Great for lunchboxes! At Revive we sell these delicious oatie bars made from the same ingredients.

Cranberry Oatie Balls

MAKES 16

½ cup Brazil nuts

½ cup rolled oats (fine)

½ coconut shredded

¼ cup cranberries dried

¼ cup honey

¼ cup tahini

1. Put the Brazil nuts in a food processor and process for 10 seconds or until they are partially blended. You want a combination of nut dust and chunks of Brazil nuts.

2. Combine all ingredients in a bowl and mix well.

3. Form into 1 tablespoon sized balls. Squish them together tightly with your fingers and then roll into balls.

4. Put on some baking paper on a baking tray and bake at 150°C (300 °F) for 25 minutes or when they start to turn brown.

5. Let them cool for 30 minutes before eating as they need to firm up.

Wet your hands before rolling to make it easier to squish the balls together.

They will store in an airtight container for at least a week.

Tahini

Tahini is ground-up sesame seeds. It is kind of like a runny peanut butter. Good for salad dressings, hummus, in stir-fries and in these nice balls. Keep some in your refrigerator. Make sure you get "unhulled" tahini - it tastes better and has a smoother texture.

While on holiday I found a "real fruit" ice cream place in Hokitika that served a cucumber version of its ice creams. I was reluctant to purchase it however a friend did, I tried it and it was amazing!! You would never think cucumber would work with ice cream. Here is a whole foods version and also I popped a little mint in which balances off the flavours a little more. Don't be scared - give it a try - you will be pleasantly surprised.

Cucumber & Mint Ice Cream

MAKES 3 X 1 CUP SERVES

2 large ripe bananas frozen

2 cups cucumber chopped and frozen

10 mint leaves

1 tablespoon liquid honey

1 cup cashew nuts

garnish: mint

garnish: cashew nuts

1. Put all ingredients into a food processor and process for 2 minutes or until smooth. You may need to add a little water or spoon down the sides to help it along.

2. Serve immediately with a garnish of mint and cashew nuts.

Store in the freezer for up to 10 minutes to stop it melting, however any longer and it will become icy.

Squeeze the honey in evenly around the food processor so it mixes well - if you just put in one blob it can stick to the sides.

This is a lovely simple and fresh dessert. Sometimes you do not need a fancy sweet, just some fresh fruit can finish a meal magnificently!

Pineapple & Mint

MAKES 4-8 SERVES

1 ripe pineapple

juice of 1 lime

4 tablespoons mint
roughly chopped

1. Peel and slice the pineapple into bite-sized slices.

2. Squeeze the lime juice over the top.

3. Chop the mint and sprinkle on top.

The key to a great dish is choosing a great pineapple. Generally a pineapple should mostly be yellow to indicate it is ripe and sweet.

I love berry smoothies but sometimes I just want something light and refreshing. Try this version which is more like a thick fruit drink than a smoothie. You can use any berry but the strawberry one is great.

Strawberry Slushy

MAKES 2 X 1 CUP SERVES

2 cups frozen strawberries

1 tablespoon lemon juice

1 tablespoon honey or date puree

1 cup water

1.   Combine all ingredients in a blender and blend until smooth.

2.   Serve immediately and garnish with mint.

You can add some mint to the blender as an optional extra.

Make sure you make it just before serving as it will melt very quickly.

This is a fresh and healthy dessert that looks amazing.

Fruit Salad with Peach Cream

MAKES 4 X 1 CUP SERVES

PEACH CREAM:

400g (12oz) tin peaches
(including juice)

1 cup cashew nuts

FRESH FRUIT OPTIONS:

watermelon

blueberries

strawberries

kiwifruit

tinned mandarins

garnish: mint

1. Put the peaches and cashew nuts into a blender and blend until smooth.

2. Pour into serving glasses, dividing evenly.

3. Chop fruit and arrange on top of the peach cream and garnish with mint.

When chopping fruit use a very sharp knife so you get clean cuts and well defined edges on the fruit. Also handle the fruit carefully. This will give the best visual appearance.

To help your fruit last longer and taste fresher keep it in the refrigerator.

I love serving this on Christmas Day. It is so silky and smooth. Just like a regular egg nog but healthier!

Vegg Nog

MAKES 2 X 1 CUP SERVES

2 large bananas frozen

¼ teaspoon vanilla essence

¼ teaspoon cinnamon

¼ teaspoon nutmeg

¼ teaspoon clove powder

1 tablespoon honey or date puree

1 cup milk of your choice

1 tablespoon tahini

garnish: sliced almonds

garnish: cinnamon sticks (optional)

1. Put all ingredients into a blender and blend until smooth.

2. Serve in nice glasses with a garnish of cinnamon and some sliced almonds.

3. Add a cinnamon stick if you want it to look extra special.

You can use any combination of your favourite spices for this drink. It will also work fine with regular bananas.

Clove Powder

Traditionally used in apple pie, cloves have a delicious flavour. Nice in many sweet and savoury dishes. I find it easier to use the powdered variety rather than having to remember to fish out the cloves.

Step-by-Step

Breakfast Bowls 178

Dahls 180

Dessert Glasses 182

Iced Drinks 184

Use this step-by-step guide to help you customise your own recipes. Simply follow the instructions to create dishes based on your favourite ingredients and the ingredients you have available at the time.

You will need a little cooking intelligence to make these work and the suggested serving sizes are a very rough guide. But give them a go and your cooking skills will quickly improve while you discover new dishes!

Check out the other Revive Cafe Cookbooks for more step-by-step guides!

Step-by-Step Breakfast Bowls

This is a great healthy cooked breakfast.

Cook and prepare each ingredient. Colour is important. Serve in individually prepared bowls for each person or put all items in the centre of the table, buffet-style.

1 Protein
heat or cook

choose 1:

black beans

baked beans

fried tofu cubes

roasted nuts (almonds, cashews)

fried tempeh cubes

chickpeas (garbanzo beans)

2 Cooked
heat or cook

choose 1 or 2:

roasted potatoes

hash browns

roasted kumara

sauteed mushrooms

courgettes (zucchini)

grilled tomatoes

steamed asparagus

3 Fresh
chop and cube

choose 1 or 2:

avocado

tomatoes

corn

370,440
different combinations

4 Grains
cook or warm

5 Garnish
apply on top

choose 1:

cooked quinoa

cooked brown rice

cooked millet

wholegrain toast

corn bread

choose 2:

parsley

coriander (cilantro)

tomato sauce or ketchup

hummus

tahini dressing (page 141)

lime wedges

lemon wedges

Step-by-Step Dahls

Dahls are a warming and delicious meal and can be prepared in one pot or pan. Serve on brown rice or quinoa.

Just keep throwing ingredients into your pot or pan in order. Make sure the lentils are cooked before finishing the dish.

1 Base
saute for 5 minutes or until onion is soft

2 Flavour
add to onion mix and stir to activate flavours

3 Legume
add and simmer for 15-45 minutes (depends which lentil)

---

add all:

1 tablespoon oil

1½ cups onion finely chopped (around 1 onion)

2 cloves garlic crushed or finely chopped

1 tablespoon ginger puree or ginger finely chopped

optional:

2 x 400g (12oz) tins crushed tomatoes

---

choose 1:

1 tablespoon Thai curry paste (green, red, Penang or yellow)

1 tablespoon curry powder

cumin, coriander, turmeric

---

optional choose 1:

1 cup brown (crimson) lentils

1 cup laird (light green) lentils

1 cup red lentils

1 cup yellow lentils

1 cup French puy lentils

1 cup urid dahl

add:

4-5 cups boiling water (more if it runs out before the lentils are cooked)

483,840
different combinations

4 Veges
add and heat until warm

5 Cream
stir through

6 Garnish
add last

choose 3:

frozen spinach

frozen peas

roasted pumpkin (butternut)

roasted kumara (sweet potato)

roasted eggplant (aubergine)

pan-fried courgettes

pan-fried mushrooms

capsicum (bell peppers)

optional choose 1:

cashew cream

coconut cream/milk

choose 1 or 2:

poppy seeds

coriander (cilantro)

parsley

mint

7 Check
for sweetness, flavour, saltiness and texture and adjust if necessary

Step-by-Step Dessert Glasses

You can make some delicious and healthy desserts with these ingredients.

Use the first 3 steps to make the bulk of the dessert. It may need time to thicken if you use chia seeds. Put into your glass or bowl and add the fruit and then garnish.

1 Base
add to a bowl

2 Liquid
mix in

3 Flavour
add and mix
(you can also blend)

choose 1 or 2:

cooked brown rice

chia seeds

cashew nuts

frozen banana

cooked quinoa

pumpkin or butternut

choose 1:

water

soy, rice, almond, oat milk

pineapple juice

apricot nectar

coconut milk or cream

(use liquids sparingly)

choose 1:

peanut butter

almond butter

tahini (sesame seed paste)

carob powder

honey or date puree

cinnamon

nutmeg

vanilla essence

3,426,416,640
different combinations

4 Glass
select your favourite

5 Fruit
add to bottom and/or
top of bowl

6 Garnish
sprinkle on top

choose 1:

short glasses

wine glasses

small white bowls

mugs

choose 3:

fresh berries (strawberries,
raspberries, blueberries,
boysenberries)

frozen berries (strawberries,
raspberries, blueberries,
boysenberries)

tinned fruit (peaches, apricots,
mandarins, pineapple, pears)

fresh fruit (watermelon, kiwifruit,
mango, lichees, feijoas
(pineapple guavas))

choose 2:

frozen berries

mint leaves

slivered almonds

crushed peanuts

shredded coconut

sesame seeds

cherries

blueberries

cashew cream

Step-by-Step Iced Drinks

You can create some lovely healthy drinks with these simple ingredients.

Just keep adding them to your jug or individual glasses.
Remember presentation is very important.

1 Base
pour into glass or jug

2 Flavour
add

Base

choose 1 or 2:

water

soda water

sparkling mineral water

orange juice

pineapple juice

apple juice

coconut water

optional:

ice cubes

Flavour

choose 1:

lemon juice

lime juice

fruit herbal tea bags (remove before serving)

ginger

star anise

cloves

84,672
different
combinations

3 **Sweet**
mix in

4 **Garnish**
add

optional choose 1:

honey

maple syrup

choose 2:

mint leaves

lemon slices

orange slices

strawberries finely diced

lime slices

cucumber slices

watermelon wedges

kiwifruit slices

Quick Guide Cooking Grains

Whole grains are high in fibre and nutrients. I prefer to cook them on the stove top.

Most grains yield approximately double their dry volume.

1. Boil water in your kettle - this will help cut time off the cooking process.
2. Put the required ratio of boiling water and grains into a pot at highest heat with the lid on.
3. Bring to the boil and then turn down and simmer (just bubbling). This is usually around ¼ heat setting.
4. Simmer for the required amount of time or until soft. If not quite cooked you can leave to sit with the lid on for another 10 minutes.
5. When the water reduces, steam vents will appear in the grains that assist with cooking. Do not stir as you will interrupt it.

Quick Guide Cooking Beans

Beans are high in protein. With a little planning, cooking your own beans is easy and you will save a lot of money.

These times are very approximate as the cooking time will vary significantly depending on the age and size of the bean.

1. Soak overnight (or at least 6 hours) in water (3 times as much water as beans).
2. Drain water and rinse in a colander or sieve.
3. Put fresh boiling water and beans into a pot and bring to boil. Simmer (just bubbling) on high heat for time specified or until soft.
4. Rinse under cold water in a colander or sieve.
5. Use straight away or put in refrigerator. Can be frozen and will defrost quickly under hot water.

Quick Guide Cooking Lentils

Lentils are high in protein and great in almost any savoury dish.

1. Lentils do not need soaking (except whole urid).
2. Bring to the boil with the amount of water indicated opposite and then turn down to simmer.
3. Cook with lid off for the approximate cooking times or until soft. Be careful as they can burn if water runs out.
4. Do not add salt until the end as this will inhibit the cooking process. Water will usually be used up but if not, drain.
5. Freeze any leftovers.

Long Grain Brown Rice - 1 cup

A great staple grain that I love to use.
Ideal for serving with hotpots.

water	simmer
2 cups	30 minutes

Buck Wheat - 1 cup

A nice soft grain good for salads. Just
add lots of flavour.

water	simmer
2 cups	20 minutes

Short Grain Brown Rice - 1 cup

Great for sticky rice salads, rice
puddings and risottos.

water	simmer
3 cups	40 minutes

Fine Couscous - 1 cup

Don't cook! Just mix with boiling water,
stir and let sit. Add turmeric for colour.

water	let sit
1 cup	5 minutes

Bulghur Wheat - 1 cup

Makes nice salads. Depending on the
size, the time may vary.

water	simmer
2 cups	20 minutes

Quinoa - 1 cup

The perfect delicious, quick cooking
grain. High in protein.

water	simmer
2 cups	12 minutes

Chickpeas - 1 cup

Our most used, favourite and delicious
bean. Also called Garbanzo Beans.

water	simmer
6 cups	40 minutes

Black Beans - 1 cup

Nice in hotpots and salads for contrast.
Also called Turtle Beans.

water	simmer
6 cups	30 minutes

Red Kidney Beans - 1 cup

Good all purpose bean. Great colour
and holds its shape well.

water	simmer
6 cups	60 minutes

Large Lima Beans - 1 cup

Amazing in salads.
Also called Butter Beans.

water	simmer
6 cups	60 minutes

Small White Beans - 1 cup

Good soft bean with a neutral flavour.
Also called Navy Beans.

water	simmer
6 cups	60 minutes

Black-Eyed Beans - 1 cup

Nice in stews and hotpots.

water	simmer
6 cups	30 minutes

Red Lentils - 1 cup

A fast-cooking staple pantry item.
Creates a delicious meal in minutes.

water	simmer
3 cups	10 minutes

Urid (Black) Lentils - 1 cup

Split urid are best. If whole you will
need to soak overnight.

water	simmer
6 cups	50 minutes

Yellow Lentils - 1 cup

Like red lentils but with a more solid
texture. Also called Toor Dahl.

water	simmer
3 cups	15 minutes

Brown (Crimson) Lentils - 1 cup

Great in lasagnes and casseroles.
Nice with sage.

water	simmer
3 cups	30 minutes

French Green Lentils - 1 cup

Cook until just soft. They retain their
shape. Also called Puy Lentils.

water	simmer
4 cups	40 minutes

Laird (Brown) Lentils - 1 cup

Often confused with brown lentils.
These need a lot of flavour.

water	simmer
3 cups	30 minutes

Salads

Cos Caesar 26
Moroccan Chickpeas 28
Seedy Slaw 30
Classic Greek Salad 32
Sweet Chilli Roast Veges 34
Mushroom Risotto Salad 36
Balsamic Lentil & Roasted Beetroot 38
Italian Chickpeas 40
Dukkah Roasted Potatoes 42
Sweet Bean Medley 44
Thai Green Curry Veges 46
Corn & Pepper Fiesta 48

Chewy Indonesian Rice 50
Thai Satay Kumara Noodles 52
Honey Mustard Roasted
   Potatoes 54
Moroccan Leek Rice 56
Almond Carrot Crunch 58
Satay Cauliflower with Peanuts 60
Spring Kumara Mingle 62
Tuscan Mesclun 64
Revive-dorf Salad 66
Pacifika Coleslaw 68

Hotpots & Stir Fries

Pumpkin, Spinach, Ginger & Tofu Curry 7?
Not Butter Chicken 74
Corn & Potato Chowder 76
Indonesian Chickpea Satay 78
Thai Red Curry with Tofu 80
Dahl Makhani 82
Dahl-a-touille 84
Malai Kofta 86
Mushroom Bhaji 88
Spanish Bean Stew 90
Revive Chilli 92
Mushroom Goulash 94

Salads

4C Salad 18
Sesame Asian Greens 20
Spiced Date Pilau 22
Revive Raw Salad 24
Cos & Courgette Mingle 26
Thai Satay Noodles 28
Israeli Couscous 30
Creamy Roasted Veges 32
Smoked Spanish Rice 34
Egyptian Rice & Lentils 36
Thai Bean Mingle 38
Pad Thai Noodle Salad 40

Bombay Roasted Potatoes 42
Mesclun Mango 44
Italian Fusilli Mingle 46
Green Salad & Almonds 48
Summer Quinoa Mingle 50
Pesto Infused Roasted Potatoes 52
Wild Green Salad 54
Greek Chickpeas 56
Italian Pumpkin Risotto 58
Kumara & Cranberry Mingle 60
Curried Black-Eyed Bean Salad 62
Baghdad Bulghur 64
Pesto Penne Pasta 66
Creamy Thai Rice Salad 68

Brussels Sprout Medley 70

Hotpots & Stir Fries

Indonesian Sadur Lodeh 74
Classic Chickpea Ratatouille 76
Thai Tofu Green Curry 78
Not Chicken Alfredo 80
Mixed Bean Jumbalaya 82
Tofu & Quinoa Stir Fry 84
Moroccan Date & Chickpea Dahl 86
Curried Poppy Seed Dahl 88
Indian Spinach & Chickpea Korma 90

Salads

Brown Rice Waldorf 16
Thai Ginger Slaw 18
Mega Cos Salad 20
Asian Ginger & Tofu Salad 22
Autumn Cauliflower Mingle 24
Blissful Sprout Medley 26
Rainbow Chickpeas 28
French Peanut Puy Lentils 30
Olivier, The Russian Salad 32
Sweet Shanghai Soy Beans 34
Tangy Leafy Salad 36
Italian Risotto 38

Apple Poppy Coleslaw 40
Caraway Kumara & Cabbage Salad 42
Basil Linguine Salad 44
Indian Curried Cauliflower
   & Chickpeas 46
Fragrant Thai Peanut Noodles 48
Quinoa & Cashew Mingle 50

Hotpots & Stir Fries

Palak Paneer 54
Penne Alfredo 56
Thai Yellow Curry 58
Peanutty Pineapple Quinoa 60
Sweet & Sour Tofu 62

Thai Massaman Lentil Casserole 64
Cauliflower & Chickpea Satay 66
Navratan Korma 68
Mediterranean Quinoa & Sauce 70
Italian Butter Bean Pasta 72
Asparagus & Quinoa Stir Fry 74
Steam Fried Veges 76
Donburi 78

Main Meals

Scrummy Stuffed Sweet Potato 82
Kumara & Carrot Cakes 84
Pumpkin & Cranberry Filo Parcels 86
Okonomiyaki (Japanese Pancake) 88

Salads

Fresh Autumn Mingle 16
Asian Quinoa Salad 18
Root Vegetable Medley 20
Asian Soba Noodles 22
Watercress & Sweet Potato 24
Tempeh & Cherry Tomato 26
Cauli-cous Salad 28
Leek & Pesto Chickpeas 30
Kale & Lentil Salad 32
Succotash 34
German Roasted Potatoes 36
Fruity Moroccan Couscous 38

Quick Tahini Coleslaw 40
Italian Tomato Rice Salad 42
Summer Spiral Pasta Salad 44
Sesame Cucumber Ribbon 46

Hotpots & Stir Fries

Chilli Con Haba 52
Aromatic Cambodian Curry 54
Tuscan Bean Casserole 56
Penang Thai Bean Curry 58
Sweet Apricot Sesame Tofu 60
Super-charged Lentil Stew 62
Thai Almond Tofu Noodles 64

Mushroom & Cashew Rice 66
Figgy Thai Chickpeas 68
Black Bean Stir Fry 70
Thai Green Curry Stir Fry 72
Mexican Quinoa 74
Cambodian Red Rice 76

Main Meals

Falafel Pita Wraps 82
Creamed Corn Baked Potato 84
Turkish Moussaka 86
Energising Mexican Feast 88
Satay Tofu Kebabs 90

Salads

Bright Butter Beans 16
Pesto Green Beans 18
Mexican Guacamole Salad 20
Tropical Summer Salad 22
Parsnip, Pear, Rocket & Pecans 24
Watercress & Potato Salad 26
Purple Power Quinoa Salad 28
Thai Green Curry Rice 30
Tangy Fennel Tofu Salad 32
Autumn Butternut Salad 34
Asian Cabbage Crunch 36
Pineapple Powered Sweet Potato 38

Hotpots & Stir Fries

Sri Lankin Balti 42
South Indian Eggplant &
   Cashew Curry 44
Chickpea Tikka Masala 46
Dahl Aloo Ghobi 48
Lentil Ragout on Potato Mash 50
Tamarind & Butternut Dahl 52
Chana Saag 54
Mexican Black Bean Casserole 56
Quinoa Stir Fry with Tempeh 58
Hot Mushroom Mingle 60
Thai Vegetable Stir Fry 62

Thai Green Curry Tofu 64
Thai Kumara Stir Fry 66
Satay Wild Rice Risotto 68
Amaranth & Root Vege Mingle 70

Main Meals

Gado Gado 76
Mini Pumpkin Frittatas 78
Mega Bean Tacos 80
Indian Sweet Potato Rosti 82
Tuscan Wholemeal Pizza 84
Indian Spinach & Potato Wrap 86
Carrot & Beet Fritters 88
Bramboracky (Czech Pancake) 90

Curried Cabbage Stir Fry 96
Kidney Bean Stir Fry 98
Quinoa Stir Fry 100
Miso Bean Mingle 102
Super Nachos 104

Main Meals

Meatless Meatballs 108
Not Chicken Burritos 110
Baked Potato with Chickpea Korma 112
Curried Zucchini Fritters 114
Neat Loaf 116
Honey & Soy Tofu Steaks 118

Spanikopita 120
Pumpkin Risotto Cake 122
Pumpkin & Kumara Balls 124
Mushroom Cannelloni 126
Shepherdess Pie 128
Indian Potato & Chickpea
   Wraps 130
Scrambled Tofu with
   Mushrooms 132

Soups

Carrot & Coriander Soup 136
Creamy Tomato Soup 138

Creamy Thai Pumpkin Soup 140
Indian Spiced Lentil Soup 142

Flavour Boosters

Sunflower Cream 146
Classic Hummus 147
Pineapple Salsa 148
Almond Dukkah 149
Revive Aioli 150
Chermoula Dressing 151
Satay Sauce 152
Italian Tomato Sauce 153
Date Puree 154

Onion Jam 155

Sweet Things

Boysenberry Nice-Cream 158
Blueberry & Cashew
   Cheesecake 160
Buckwheat Hotcakes w Pear Cream 162
Apricot Oat Slice 164
Blueberry Smoothie 166
Banana Date Smoothie 167
Boysenberry Rice Pudding 168
5 Grain Breakfast 170
Bircher Muesli 172

Tarka Dahl 92
Hearty Lentil Casserole 94
Chilli Con Tofu 96
Thai Massaman Peanut Curry 98
Thai Green Curry Lentils 100
Italian White Bean Stew 102
Tuscan Brown Lentils 104
Asian Peanut Stir Fry 106
Mediterranean Chickpea Stir Fry 108
Herbed Lentil & Quinoa Stir Fry 110
Indian Rice Pilaf 112

Main Meals

Baked Thai Corn Cakes 116
Tuscan White Bean Wraps 118
Revive Roast Vege Frittata 120
Greek Potato & Feta Cake 122
Thai Tofu Curry Pie 124
Lentil & Vegetable Lasagne 126
Curried Potato Cakes 128
Indian Curried Filo Pie 130
Chickpea Pizza 132
Beefless Burgers 134
Tuscan White Bean Cannelloni 136
Traditional Corn Fritters 138

Flavour Boosters

Healthy Basil Pesto 142
Chick Bread 144
Avocado Guacamole 146
Root-beet Dip 148
Red Pepper Pesto 149
Revive Relish 150
White Cashew Sauce 152
Tomato Salsa 153
Ravishing Red Bean Dip 154
Lemon Dressing 156

Sweet Things

Bliss Balls 160
Revive Muesli (Granola) 162
Whipped Cashew Cream 164
Classic Strawberry Smoothie 165
Almond Milk 166
Boysenberry Smoothie 168
Tropical Fruit Salad 169
Hot Honey, Lemon & Ginger Soother 170
Porridge (Oatmeal) 172
Mango Smoothie 174
Carob Ice 175
Muesli Smoothie 176

Vegetable Pakoras 90
Broccoli Infused Flatbread 92
Summer Burger 94
Smoked Stuffed Peppers 96
Pesto & Potato Chickbread Pizza 98
Courgette & Cauliflower Bake 100
Thai Spring Rolls 102

Soups

Mexican Black Bean Soup 108
Vietnamese Pho Noodles 110
Lentil & Beetroot Borscht 112
Broccoli & Dill Soup 114
Lentil & Kumara Soup 116

Leek & Potato Soup 118

Flavour Boosters

Cheezy Cashew Sauce 122
Basil Hummus 124
Nutty Capsicum Dip 124
Sparkling Lime Juice 126
Almost Egg Spread 128
Thai Ginger Dressing 130
Tofu Mayo 132
Almond Butter 133

Breakfasts

Power Oat Breakfast 138
Nearly French Toast 140
Warming Millet Porridge 142
Buckwheat Waffles 144
Butternut Oatmeal 146
Golden Omelette 148
Portobello Mushrooms 150

Sweet Things

Plum & Ginger Slice 154

Apricot Bliss Balls 156
Better Than Ice Cream 158
Pineapple Rice Pudding 160
Black Almond Fudge 162
Peanut Butter Smoothie 164
Blueberry, Apple Crumble 166
Pumpkin Pie 168
Honest Pina Colada 170
Banana Split 172
Coconut & Date Fudge 174

Tamale Pie 92
Thai Infused Baked Potatoes 94
Reuben Burger 96
Mushroom & Leek Risotto 98

Soups

Chunky Vegetable & Lentil 102
Creamy & Minty Pea Soup 104
Mushroom & Thyme Soup 106
Satay Sweet Potato Bisque 108
Minestrone 110
Malaysian Laksa 112
Curried Cauliflower Soup 114

Sides

Mediterranean Vegetables 120
Honey Glazed Carrots 122
Traditional Potato Mash 123
Sweet Potato Fries 124
Garlic Mushrooms 126
Broccoli & Cranberries 127
Satay Green Beans 128
Smoked Wedges 130
Green Pea Mingle 131
Cauliflower Cheese 132
Tangy Coriander Rice 134
Roasted Beetroot 135

Breakfast Vegetables 136

Sweet Things

Blueberry Parfait 140
Rainbow Fruit Kebabs 142
Healthy Banoffee Pie 144
Sticky Rice Mango 146
Chewy Cranberry Oat Slice 148
Blueberries & Cashew 150
Jeremy's Quinoa Breakfast 152
Moorish Carrot Cake Balls 154
Not Chocolate Mousse 156
Raspberry & Mint Smoothie 158

Sublime Green Smoothie 160
Mango & Lime Shake 161

Flavour Boosters

Mexican Salsa 164
Asian Sesame Miso 165
Moroccan Hummus 166
Homemade Sweet Chilli 168
Baba Ganoush 170
Tahini Dressing 171
Thai Red Curry Paste 172
Thai Green Curry Paste 173

Butternut Mac Cheese 92
Chunky Italian Tomato Pasta 94
Green Vegetable Cakes 96
Mexican Bean Enchilada 98

Soups

Hearty Dark Legume Soup 102
Mexican Green Pepper Soup 104
Roast Vege Soup with Dukkah 106
Tom Yum Soup 108
Old School Vegetable Soup 110
Chunky Chickpea Soup 112

Sides

Colcannon 118
Rainbow Vegetables 120
Bruschetta 121
Chunky Penang Thai Tofu 122
Bubble & Squeak 124
Sweet Potato Hash 126
Tomato & Zucchini Mingle 127

Flavour Boosters

Carrot & Coriander Dip 130
Green Pea Dip 132
Buttery Spread 133

Kalamata Olive Dressing 134
Indonesian Peanut Dip 135
Tzatziki 136
Parmeshew Cheese Sprinkle 137

Breakfasts

Supercharged Breakfast Bowl 144
Oat Waffles with Wild Berries 146
Amazing Thai Scrambled Tofu 148
Blueberry Power Breakfast Shake 150
Feijoa Buckwheat Pancakes 152
Homemade Natural Muesli 154
Naked Strawberry Jam 156
Super Quick Rice Breakfast 158

Sweet Things

Chia Seed Choc Pudding 162
Homemade Lemonade Quencher 164
Energiser Smoothie 165
Cranberry Oatie Balls 166
Cucumber & Mint Ice Cream 168
Pineapple & Mint 170
Strawberry Slushy 171
Fruit Salad with Peach Cream 172
Vegg Nog 174

Recipe Index

A

Aioli, Revive 138
Aloo Ghobi, Dahl 48
Amaranth & Root Vege Mingle 70
Amazing Thai Scrambled Tofu 148
Asian Cabbage Crunch 36
Autumn Butternut Salad 34

B

Balls, Cranberry Oatie 166
Balti, Sri Lankin 42
Basil Pesto 139
Bean Casserole, Mexican Black 56
Bean Enchilada, Mexican 98
Bean Tacos, Mega 80
Beans, Bright Butter 16
Beans, Pesto Green 18
Beet Fritters, Carrot & 88
Berries, Oat Waffles with Wild 146
Black Bean Casserole, Mexican 56
Blueberry Power Breakfast Shake 150
Bowl, Supercharged Breakfast 144
Bramboracky, Czech Pancake 90
Breakfast Bowl, Supercharged 144
Breakfast Shake, Blueberry Power 150
Breakfast, Super Quick Rice 158
Bright Butter Beans 16
Bruschetta 121
Bubble & Squeek 124
Buckwheat Pancakes, Feijoa 152
Butter Beans, Bright 16
Butternut Dahl, Tamarind & 52
Butternut Mac Cheese 92
Butternut Salad, Autumn 34
Buttery Spread 133

C

Cabbage Crunch, Asian 36
Cakes, Green Vegetable 96
Carrot & Beet Fritters 88
Carrot & Coriander Dip 130
Cashew Cream 140
Cashew Curry, South Indian, Eggplant 44
Casserole, Mexican Black Bean 56
Chana Saag 54
Cheese, Butternut Mac 92

Cheese Sprinkle, Parmeshew 137
Chia Seed Choc Pudding 162
Chickpea Soup, Chunky 112
Chickpea Tikka Masala 46
Choc Pudding, Chia Seed 162
Chunky Chickpea Soup 112
Chunky Italian Tomato Pasta 94
Chunky Penang Thai Tofu 122
Classic Hummus 141
Colcannon 118
Coriander Dip, Carrot & 130
Cranberry Oatie Balls 166
Cream, Cashew 140
Cream, Cucumber & Mint Ice 168
Cream, Fruit Salad with Peach 172
Crunch, Asian Cabbage 36
Cucumber & Mint Ice Cream 168
Curry Rice, Thai Green 30
Curry, South Indian Eggplant & Cashew 44
Curry Tofu, Thai Green 64
Czech Pancake, Bramboracky 90

D

Dahl Aloo Ghobi 48
Dahl, Tamarind & Butternut 52
Dark Legume Soup, Hearty 102
Date Puree 139
Dip, Carrot & Coriander 130
Dip, Green Pea 132
Dip, Indonesian Peanut 135
Dressing, Kalamata Olive 134
Dressing, Tahini 141
Dukkah, Roast Vege Soup with 106
Dukkah, Turkish 140

E

Eggplant & Cashew Curry, South Indian 44
Enchilada, Mexican Bean 98
Energiser Smoothie 165

F

Feijoa Buckwheat Pancakes 152
Fennel Tofu Salad, Tangy 32
Frittatas, Mini Pumpkin 78
Fritters, Carrot & Beet 88
Fruit Salad with Peach Cream 172

G

Gado Gado 76
Ghobi, Dahl Aloo 48
Green Beans, Pesto 18
Green Curry Rice, Thai 30
Green Curry Tofu, Thai 64
Green Pea Dip 132
Green Pepper Soup, Mexican 104
Green Vegetable Cakes 96
Guacamole Salad, Mexican 20

H

Hash, Sweet Potato 126
Hearty Dark Legume Soup 102
Homemade Lemonade Quencher 164
Homemade Natural Muesli 154
Hot Mushroom Mingle 60
Hummus, Classic 141

I

Ice Cream, Cucumber & Mint 168
Indian Spinach & Potato Wrap 86
Indian Sweet Potato Rosti 82
Indonesian Peanut Dip 135
Italian Tomato Pasta, Chunky 94
Italian Tomato Sauce 138

J

Jam, Naked Strawberry 156

K

Kalamata Olive Dressing 134
Kumara Stir Fry, Thai 66

L

Legume Soup, Hearty Dark 102
Lemonade Quencher, Homemade 164
Lentil Ragout on Potato Mash 50

M

Mac Cheese, Butternut 92
Masala, Chickpea Tikka 46
Mash, Lentil Ragout on Potato 50
Mega Bean Tacos 80
Mexican Bean Enchilada 98
Mexican Black Bean Casserole 56
Mexican Green Pepper Soup 104
Mexican Guacamole Salad 20

Mingle, Amaranth & Root Vege 70
Mingle, Hot Mushroom 60
Mingle, Tomato & Zucchini 127
Mini Pumpkin Frittatas 78
Mint Ice Cream, Cucumber & 168
Mint, Pineapple & 170
Muesli, Homemade Natural 154
Mushroom Mingle, Hot 60

N

Naked Strawberry Jam 156
Natural Muesli, Homemade 154
Nog, Vegg 174

O

Oat Waffles with Wild Berries 146
Oatie Balls, Cranberry 166
Old School Vegetable Soup 110
Olive Dressing, Kalamata 134

P

Pancake, Bramboracky Czech 90
Pancakes, Feijoa Buckwheat 152
Parmeshew Cheese Sprinkle 137
Parsnip, Pear, Rocket & Pecans 24
Pasta, Chunky Italian Tomato 94
Pea Dip, Green 132
Peach Cream, Fruit Salad with 172
Peanut Dip, Indonesian 135
Pear, Rocket & Pecans, Parsnip, 24
Pecans, Parsnip, Pear, Rocket & 24
Penang Thai Tofu, Chunky 122
Pepper Soup, Mexican Green 104
Pesto, Basil 139
Pesto Green Beans 18
Pineapple & Mint 170
Pineapple Powered Sweet Potato 38
Pizza, Tuscan Wholemeal 84
Potato Mash, Lentil Ragout on 50
Potato Rosti, Indian Sweet 82
Potato Salad, Watercress & 26
Potato Wrap, Indian Spinach & 86
Power Breakfast Shake, Blueberry 150
Power Quinoa Salad, Purple 28
Powered Sweet Potato, Pineapple 38
Pudding, Chia Seed Choc 162
Pumpkin Frittatas, Mini 78
Puree, Date 139
Purple Power Quinoa Salad 28

Q

Quencher, Homemade Lemonade 164
Quick Rice Breakfast, Super 158

Quinoa Salad, Purple Power 28
Quinoa Stir Fry with Tempeh 58

R

Ragout on Potato Mash, Lentil 50
Rainbow Vegetables 120
Revive Aioli 138
Rice Breakfast, Super Quick 158
Rice Risotto, Satay Wild 68
Rice, Thai Green Curry 30
Risotto, Satay Wild Rice 68
Roast Vege Soup with Dukkah 106
Rocket & Pecans, Parsnip, Pear, 24
Root Vege Mingle, Amaranth & 70
Rosti, Indian Sweet Potato 82

S

Saag, Chana 54
Salad, Autumn Butternut 34
Salad, Mexican Guacamole 20
Salad, Purple Power Quinoa 28
Salad, Tangy Fennel Tofu 32
Salad, Tropical Summer 22
Salad, Watercress & Potato 26
Salad with Peach Cream, Fruit 172
Satay Wild Rice Risotto 68
Sauce, Italian Tomato 138
School Vegetable Soup, Old 110
Scrambled Tofu, Amazing Thai 148
Seed Choc Pudding, Chia 162
Shake, Blueberry Power Breakfast 150
Slushy, Strawberry 171
Smoothie, Energiser 165
Soup, Chunky Chickpea 112
Soup, Hearty Dark Legume 102
Soup, Mexican Green Pepper 104
Soup, Old School Vegetable 110
Soup, Tom Yum 108
Soup with Dukkah, Roast Vege 106
South Indian Eggplant & Cashew Curry 44
Spinach & Potato Wrap, Indian 86
Spread, Buttery 133
Sprinkle, Parmeshew Cheese 137
Squeak, Bubble & 124
Sri Lankin Balti 42
Stir Fry, Thai Kumara 66
Stir Fry, Thai Vegetable 62
Stir Fry with Tempeh, Quinoa 58
Strawberry Jam, Naked 156
Strawberry Slushy 171
Summer Salad, Tropical 22
Super Quick Rice Breakfast 158

Supercharged Breakfast Bowl 144
Sweet Potato Hash 126
Sweet Potato, Pineapple Powered 38
Sweet Potato Rosti, Indian 82

T

Tacos, Mega Bean 80
Tahini Dressing 141
Tamarind & Butternut Dahl 52
Tangy Fennel Tofu Salad 32
Tempeh, Quinoa Stir Fry with 58
Thai Green Curry Rice 30
Thai Green Curry Tofu 64
Thai Kumara Stir Fry 66
Thai Scrambled Tofu, Amazing 148
Thai Tofu, Chunky Penang 122
Thai Vegetable Stir Fry 62
Tikka Masala, Chickpea 46
Tofu, Amazing Thai Scrambled 148
Tofu, Chunky Penang Thai 122
Tofu Salad, Tangy Fennel 32
Tofu, Thai Green Curry 64
Tom Yum Soup 108
Tomato Pasta, Chunky Italian 94
Tomato Sauce, Italian 138
Tomato & Zucchini Mingle 127
Tropical Summer Salad 22
Turkish Dukkah 140
Tuscan Wholemeal Pizza 84
Tzatziki 136

V

Vege Mingle, Amaranth & Root 70
Vege Soup with Dukkah, Roast 106
Vegetable Cakes, Green 96
Vegetable Soup, Old School 110
Vegetables, Rainbow 120
Vegetable Stir Fry, Thai 62
Vegg Nog 174

W

Waffles with Wild Berries, Oat 146
Watercress & Potato Salad 26
Wholemeal Pizza, Tuscan 84
Wild Berries, Oat Waffles with 146
Wild Rice Risotto, Satay 68
Wrap, Indian Spinach & Potato 86

Y

Yum Soup, Tom 108

Z

Zucchini Mingle, Tomato & 127